# TRUE HISTORY

## INDIGENOUS AMERICA

D1052319

### BY LIAM McDONALD

SERIES CREATED BY JENNIFER SABIN

**PENGUIN WORKSHOP**

PENGUIN WORKSHOP
An imprint of Penguin Random House LLC, New York

First published in the United States of America by Penguin Workshop,
an imprint of Penguin Random House LLC, New York, 2022

Text copyright © 2022 by Jennifer Sabin
Cover illustration copyright © 2022 by Steffi Walthall

Photo insert credits: Delia Deschamp and her family: Liam McDonald; Map: © 2022 by
Penguin Random House LLC, art by Sophie Erb; Carlisle Indian Industrial School: (Dakota
boys) National Archives photo no. 519135, (Band) National Archives photo no. 518927; 1911
Advertisement: Printed Ephemera Collection (Library of Congress) LCCN 2015657622;
Propaganda in Art: Harry T. Peters "America on Stone" Lithography Collection, National
Museum of American History, Smithsonian Institution; Propaganda in Print: National
Portrait Gallery, Smithsonian Institution; Zitkála-Šá: National Portrait Gallery, Smithsonian
Institution; The Execution of Thirty-Eight Dakota Native Americans: Harry T. Peters
"America on Stone" Lithography Collection, National Museum of American History,
Smithsonian Institution.

Visit us online at penguinrandomhouse.com.

Library of Congress Cataloging-in-Publication Data is available.

Manufactured in Canada

ISBN 9780593386088                    10 9 8 7 6 5 4 3 2 1 FRI

Design by Sophie Erb

# CONTENTS

## PART 4: RESILIENCE

# FOREWORD
## A NOTE FROM THE AUTHOR

"Be proud you're an Indian. But be careful who you tell."

This is a common phrase young Native children are taught in America, and it is one of the first things I learned from my dad about being Native. Being some of the first people to experience colonization in the United States, we hold the long memory of its brutality. The culture was forced underground, and our people survived a genocide.

My father was born in Watertown, New York, in the St. Lawrence River Valley. His family is Kanien'kehá:ka, more commonly known as Mohawk. The Mohawk are the keepers of the eastern door of the Haudenosaunee Confederacy, otherwise known as the Iroquois Confederacy (you'll learn more about this in Chapter 1). My family originates from the Kanien'kehá:ka Mohawk reserve outside of Montreal, Canada; the people are also referred to as French Mohawks or Catholic Mohawks. This name comes from their conversion to Catholicism, when Jesuit priests established the first Catholic mission in a Native village in North America in the seventeenth century.

My great-great-great-grandmother, Delia Deschamp (maiden name Warner), was born near Kahnawake Mohawk reserve, outside Quebec, Canada, in the late 1800s.

Delia's father died when she was only two years old. Like many Native children in the late 1800s, Delia was forcibly removed from her mother, Susan Sawyer, and adopted into a white household. Delia was part of what we call the "Stolen Generation," where many Native children in Canada and the United States were kidnapped from their families and put up for adoption by the government and Catholic church, and subsequently placed in white households.

After the death of her first husband, Susan would later marry a Mohawk man named Francois Robidoux, who was born on Akwesasne, a Mohawk Nation territory. Together,

Susan and Francois began a family. The Robidoux family and I can trace our shared lineage records through the same ancestor: Susan Sawyer. Our records also show that Susan's father, Louis Sawyer Sr., was buried on Akwesasne. Today, the Robidoux family continues to live there.

According to marriage records, Delia initially lived on Wolfe Island in Ontario, Canada, with her husband, and they would ultimately settle in Watertown, New York. Later in her life, Delia reconnected with her mother, Susan, and the rest of her Native family. (To see a picture of Delia and Susan, go to the photo insert.)

Even as an adult, with her deep connection to her spirituality, Delia went by the white name given to her as a child and was known to completely deny any Native ancestry when asked. She learned at a young age what kind of persecution went along with being Native.

Most Native American families today have ancestors who were subject to child separation and/or forced attendance to residential schools. Our families still carry the scars of those experiences to this day. Today my family honors Delia by carrying on her name. Some of her descendants, like my sister, are named after her. This is a way to not only recognize our heritage, but also to remember her and her experiences.

In this book, I will not shy away from the truth, for it has been willfully ignored for far too long. You will learn about the massacres, murders, and other atrocities committed against the Indigenous peoples of this country. You will learn about the strategic and coordinated efforts of the United States government to exterminate the cultural identities of Native Americans who survived. But you will also learn about the resilience of Native Americans. How despite generations of oppression and marginalization, Native American people have had profound influences on American popular culture, music, and politics. And you will soon see just how intertwined Indigenous history and knowledge is with the creation and expansion of the United States.

Today, most Americans' understanding of what it means to be Native American comes only from portrayals in Hollywood films and other media misrepresentations. This is just one small part of the large-scale coordinated genocide and ethnocide (two terms you'll learn more about in coming chapters) that continue for Indigenous people to this day. Throughout this book, I hope to present you with the truth about Native Americans, our history, and our modern culture. And I hope you will better recognize the invisibility of Native people in today's society, and ensure we are not simply thought of as a people of the past.

This book is dedicated to all the young readers out there who have always felt like their stories were missing from the history books. More specifically, this book is dedicated to Native youths who have ever felt misrepresented, underrepresented, or not represented at all within the education system. The future will be Indigenized, and you are the future.

# INTRODUCTION
## A NOTE FROM
## PROFESSOR DOUG KIEL

*Kiel is a citizen of the Oneida Nation
and teaches history at Northwestern University.*

When I was in fifth grade, we watched *Dances with Wolves* (1990) in my social studies class, and that was meant to be our education in Native American history. If you're not familiar with the film, don't be in a hurry to watch it. It stars Kevin Costner, who is also a lead actor in the TV series *Yellowstone* (2018), sporting a regrettable mullet hairdo. *Dances with Wolves* had been celebrated as a turning point in Hollywood portrayals of Native Americans, and it won an Oscar for Best Picture at the Academy Awards in 1991. Although the film featured beautiful landscapes and compelling performances— Oneida actor Graham Greene was nominated for an Oscar as

Best Supporting Actor!—the story wasn't really about Native Americans. It was about Costner's character, a white soldier in the Union Army during the Civil War, and his desire to see "the western frontier" of the Great Plains and its Native people before they disappeared (or so he imagined). Along the way, Costner's character makes new friends, learns how to speak Lakota, and falls in love with a white woman who had been taken captive as a child. In sum, it is a story about two white people and Native people are simply the backdrop. The same thing has often happened in history books! The late Dakota philosopher Vine Deloria Jr. referred to this as the "cameo theory," in which US history is presented as primarily a story about European Americans, and Indigenous people are in the background with everyone else.

The book you hold in your hands is quite special. Liam McDonald's book is one of too few that provides young readers with Indigenous perspectives on North America's history. You now have a *much* better resource for studying Native American history than I did as a young student.

I am a citizen of the Oneida Nation, which is "Younger Brother" to the Mohawk Nation, in the Haudenosaunee (Iroquois) Confederacy. In the pages ahead, you will learn about our confederacy of six nations, a sophisticated democratic government that predates the United States by centuries. Not only have Haudenosaunee ideas played an important role in shaping the North American way of life, they also have much to contribute to our shared future. In an era of climate crisis, for instance, the Seventh Generation philosophy is a model for sustainability. In our oral tradition, a leader known as the Peacemaker taught us the Great Law of Peace, part of which includes the responsibility to make decisions that assure the well-being of our people seven generations into the future. How long is that? It's over two hundred years! Haudenosaunee philosophy encourages us to be mindful of the relationship between our present lives and the distant future.

*Indigenous America* addresses a variety of topics that you would expect to find in a Native American history book. You will read some truth-telling about a legacy of genocide, and how the US legal system justified the theft of Indigenous lands by characterizing Native Americans as inferior people. Religious institutions likewise labeled Native Americans as inferior, and on this basis, generations of Native children were forcibly removed from their families and sent to distant boarding schools to have their language and culture ripped away from them. Even when describing the worst traumas of the past, Liam McDonald reminds readers that Native people have never been passive victims; they have always actively fought for their own interests. Gerald Vizenor, a White Earth Ojibwe author, coined the term "survivance" to link the twin efforts of survival and resistance. The American Indian Movement (AIM) founded in Minneapolis, Minnesota, in response to local police brutality in the 1960s, is one such activist organization whose role in Native American history you will learn about.

In addition to highlighting this spirit of survivance, this book highlights Native American brilliance. The value of Indigenous knowledge has been historically underappreciated. Few kids in elementary school, for instance, learn about the great Indigenous city of Cahokia in present-day Illinois, near St. Louis, Missouri. Cahokia was a large and important urban center in the precolonial world, yet this and other archaeological sites have been disrespected or even bulldozed. *Indigenous America* tells the story of Sequoyah and his invention of a Cherokee language alphabet. Lastly, since the author, Liam, is also a musician, this volume in the True History series also speaks to the contributions that Indigenous people have made to popular American music. You may have already heard Native American musicians and didn't even know it—keep reading to find out who they are! As you enjoy *Indigenous America*, keep in mind that developing a complex understanding of Native American history is not just about the past, it's about your future, too. As Indigenous nations today reclaim lands that were taken from them illegally, and continue to develop the strength of their own tribal governmental institutions, it will be crucial to understand the events of the past in order to make sense of Indigenous-US relations in the future.

# CHAPTER 1
## THE HAUDENOSAUNEE CONFEDERACY

On June 11, 1776, two groups of people living on the same land converged under one roof in Philadelphia, Pennsylvania, for a meeting. One group was the Indigenous people who had been living on the land for time immemorial, meaning so long ago that humans have no record or memory of it. The other group consisted of white men of European descent who, in historically relative terms, had only very recently arrived on the land. Most of these men could trace their immediate roots directly back to Great Britain, a country across the Atlantic Ocean.

The European men were preparing to draft a document

that would declare their independence from Great Britain. They believed the king was tyrannical, meaning he governed the people through oppressive rule. Because of this, they wanted to establish their own nation: the United States of America. Their nation would be a free, independent land— one that they would govern, not some king overseas.

Why, then, were these two very different groups of people meeting just days before the founding of the United States of America?

That day in Philadelphia, there was a meeting of the Second Continental Congress at Independence Hall. The Congress was the group of delegates, or representatives, from the thirteen colonies in America that united during the Revolutionary War, which had begun just a year prior, in 1775. These delegates were the ones in charge of drafting the documents that would soon define their new government: the Declaration of Independence and the US Constitution. The president of Congress was John Hancock. He was the one who had invited the Indigenous people, who were all members of the Haudenosaunee Confederacy.

Inside Independence Hall, Hancock stood across from the chiefs of the Haudenosaunee Confederacy. These chiefs, or "Hoyane," as they called themselves, were the highest members of a league of six Native American nations that the Europeans called the Iroquois.

## WHAT'S THAT WORD?

**Haudenosaunee** (say: hoh-dee-noh-SHOW-nee) in English translates to "the people of the longhouse," after the large structures they built to house their families, called *longhouses*. When the original five tribal nations—the Mohawk, the Oneida, the Onondaga, the Cayuga, and the Seneca—agreed to a peace alliance, this created the Haudenosaunee Confederacy, which is sometimes called the Iroquois Confederacy (more on this in Chapter 2).

**Iroquois** (say: ear-oh-kwa) is derived from the Algonquin (a different Indigenous language) word *Irinakhoiw*, which translates to "snake." In this book, we have chosen to use the word *Haudenosaunee*, as this is the original name for their people.

In fact, the illustration on this book's cover is a representation of that very meeting. The Haudenosaunee Confederacy was the first independent power to recognize the legitimacy of the Second Continental Congress as a national government through a peace treaty the year before.

The members of Congress had invited the Haudenosaunee chiefs to publicly announce their neutrality and friendship. We know this because all the daily proceedings were recorded in the Journals of the Continental Congress. Hancock had even prepared a speech to show his appreciation of the chiefs. On the floor of Independence Hall, Hancock declared, "Brothers, We hope the friendship that is between you and us will be firm, and continue as long as the sun shall shine, and the waters run, that we and you may be as one people, and have but one heart, and be kind to one another as brethren."

To reciprocate Hancock's kind words, a chief from the Onondaga Nation performed the ritual ceremony of granting Hancock a Native name: Karanduaan, meaning "Great Tree" in their language. This name was a reference to the Great Tree of Peace, which in Haudenosaunee history referred to the peace that brought the original five nations together. The Great Tree of Peace symbolizes that peace can grow if you nurture it. (You'll read more about this in the next chapter.)

The name given to Hancock was no light gesture. It shows that the chiefs envisioned their friendship and neutrality to have roots as deep as a tree.

Only days after the Haudenosaunee chiefs arrived,

## WHAT'S IN A NAME?

### Conotocarius

Though the chiefs gave John Hancock a name that reflected their good-standing relationship, this wasn't always the case. In 1753, shortly before the French and Indian War, military leader George Washington (the future first president of the United States) met with members from the Seneca and Oneida tribes to discuss how they might assist Washington with encroaching French forces. Sometime after or during these discussions, the Seneca and Oneida leaders gave Washington a name, Conotocarius, meaning "devourer of villages" or "town taker." The name was a reference to Washington's great-grandfather John, who, like George, had a long history and reputation of colonizing Native lands and communities.

Congress formed a committee to formally draft the Declaration of Independence. This Committee of Five, as it was known, was made up of Thomas Jefferson, Benjamin

Franklin, John Adams, Robert R. Livingston, and Roger Sherman. These were some of the men we now refer to as the Founders. With the Haudenosaunee chiefs inside the halls of Congress on the eve of American independence, the impact and influence of Haudenosaunee ideas on the Founders is unmistakable.

In the Declaration, which was intended for the king of Great Britain, the committee lists twenty-seven grievances. These were all the problems they had with the king, and their reasons for breaking free from his rule. Thomas Jefferson, a Virginian who would later become the third president of the United States, was tasked to write much of the Declaration. Jefferson wrote this as the final grievance: "He [the king] has excited domestic insurrections amongst us, and has endeavored to bring on the inhabitants of our frontiers, the merciless Indian Savages, whose known rule of warfare, is an undistinguished destruction of all ages, sexes and conditions."

## WHAT'S THAT WORD?

**Savage** comes from the old French word *sauvage*, which means untamed and wild. The word can be traced back even further to Latin where it means "of the woods." It is a racial slur that labels people as ferocious and undomesticated, needing to be civilized.

On July 4, 1776, just twenty-three days after John Hancock and the Haudenosaunee chiefs had met to publicly announce their friendship, the Declaration of Independence was signed. And in this document that declared that "all men are created equal," the Indigenous people who had been living on the land for countless generations, including the Haudenosaunee chiefs, were cast as the enemies of the Founders and America.

With the stroke of a pen, Thomas Jefferson, along with the other men who signed the Declaration of Independence, would forever cast Indigenous people into the margins of the new nation's origin story. In the eyes of the Founders, the Natives were no more than "savage" allies of the tyrannical king of Great Britain. Ironically, as you'll soon learn, these men would prove to be far more oppressive than the king.

You may have heard a teacher or an adult say that the United States is a "great experiment" or how the Founders possessed great foresight and wisdom for their creation of a unique government. While that is certainly true, it is not the full picture. These men had a vision for their future—one that didn't include Natives. This is because, above all, these men were after one thing: land. The Haudenosaunee and other Indigenous people living on the land were physical and figurative obstacles that, in the coming years, white European settlers would need to overcome to control and claim the land as their own.

This quest for land was part of a larger coordinated effort by the United States government. A strategy not only to erase and eradicate the Indigenous people, but to simultaneously portray them as a sub-human, 'savage' race not subject to the laws and protections outlined in the Declaration of Independence and the Constitution. This, of course, was a myth—or a falsehood. And it would be just one of many used against Native Americans in an attempt to disparage them and minimize their role within the future of the new country.

In the following pages, we aim to explain the true history of the Indigenous people of North America—who they are and what they stand for—and how the United States government has attempted to erase and rewrite their story.

This is our story.

# CHAPTER 2
## THE STORY OF THE GREAT PEACEMAKER

You probably learned that Christopher Columbus discovered America in 1492. This, too, is a myth, which we'll discuss more in Chapter 6. We know this because for tens of thousands of years prior to Columbus's arrival, Indigenous people were living on the continent of North America. They lived as far north as the snow-covered hills that are now present-day Canada and as far south as the coastal shores of present-day Mexico.

There were many different tribal nations and confederacies sprawled across North and South America, like the Aztec, Maya, and Inca, which you may have heard about.

## WHAT'S THE (RIGHT) WORD?

Native American or Indigenous people? You may have heard both terms used before and both are correct, depending on who you ask. A quick history: The term *Native American* grew in popularity during political movements in the 1960s and 70s. As you'll soon learn, Native Americans were living in North America long before Christopher Columbus arrived and they did not call the land America. So the term is a bit misleading. For this reason, many people prefer the term *Indigenous* (with a capital I), meaning original inhabitant of a land. Still, some people refer to themselves as Native or Indian and most prefer to be known by their tribal affiliation, like Mohawk, Cherokee, or Seneca, for example. In Canada, which is part of North America, terms like First Nations and First Peoples are preferred. In Central and South America, Spanish speakers prefer the encompassing term *indígenas* (indigenous). So while both Native American and Indigenous people/person are correct, it's always best to ask someone how they'd prefer to be addressed. In this book, we use the terms interchangeably.

But there were also five tribal nations who lived along the Great Lakes, the five large, interconnected freshwater lakes in the upper region between what is now the United States and Canada. Though they lived in proximity, the five nations—the Mohawk, the Oneida, the Onondaga, the Cayuga, and the Seneca—engaged in long periods of deadly violence against one another.

## THE NATIONS OF THE HAUDENOSAUNEE CONFEDERACY

**The Mohawk**, *Kanien'kehá:ka*, "the people of the flint."

**The Oneida**, *Onyota'a:ka*, "the people of the standing stone."

**The Onondaga**, *Onöñda'gaga'*, "the people of the hills"; also "the keepers of the fire" because they are the most centrally located nation situated between the Oneida and Cayuga nations.

**The Cayuga**, *Gayogohó:no'*, "the people of the great swamp."

**The Seneca**, *Onödowága*, "the great hill people."

**The Tuscarora**, *Skarù:rę*, "hemp-gatherers" or "shirt-wearing people," were later accepted into the confederacy, in 1722.

(To see a full map of their present-day locations, go to the photo insert.)

This tribal warfare lasted until the visionary leader known as the Great Peacemaker brought the Great Law of Peace to the tribes, ceasing the infighting and uniting the five nations. The story of the Great Peacemaker is one of the most powerful epic stories in Native American oral tradition, meaning history that is passed down from one generation to the next through spoken word, not written. The Great Law of Peace would become the constitution of the Haudenosaunee Confederacy. Similar to the oral story of the Great Peacemaker, the Great Law of Peace was not recorded by written language. Instead, it was recorded on wampum belts, which were strung together by black, purple, and white beads made from shells, typically quahog clam shells.

The origin story of the Haudenosaunee Confederacy and the Great Peacemaker is one filled with symbols and traditions that would ultimately find their way into the written history of the United States, and even inform the US Constitution.

## II. The Great Peacemaker

The story begins with the Creator, the ultimate creator of everything within the universe and the Giver of Life. The Creator was unhappy with the five tribes because of the continued infighting. So the Creator sent a young boy from the Huron nation to spread a message of peace to the warring tribes. Even as a child, people knew the boy was special because he always spoke of peace. Many considered him to be a prophet.

When he was ready to spread his message, this boy, the Great Peacemaker, crafted a canoe entirely out of white stone, a symbol of peace. The Creator believed the Haudenosaunee leaders were the ones responsible for the so-called dark times, these periods of violence. He believed they used evil sorcery to achieve their positions of power. So the Great Peacemaker decided to seek out these evil leaders first. While he was searching, he came across a woman named Jikonhsaseh, who was known to provide resources to warriors and enable the fighting between tribes.

The Great Peacemaker told her of his message. Jikonhsaseh became the first person to accept the Great Peace. He then went to the Mohawk in the east. They were hesitant to agree to the Great Peace for fear it was a trap. But the Great Peacemaker spoke of the power that would come from the many tribes moving as one. And, after putting the Great Peacemaker to a test, the Mohawk were the first tribe to agree to the Great Peace.

As he made his way west, the message of the Great Peace grew. One by one, the most powerful and evil men agreed to end the bloodshed. One of the last holdouts was a feared Onondaga leader named Tadodaho, a man so venomous and evil that snakes grew out of his hair. Another warrior named Hiawatha had previously spoken of peace to Tadodaho, and he had killed Hiawatha's entire family.

In a state of despair, Hiawatha went to a lake where he found purple and white shells on the shore. He began stringing them together. This brought him peace once again. He then joined the Great Peacemaker to continue to spread the message. Four of the five nations had agreed, but there was one nation left that had yet to accept the peace: the Onondaga. Members of the four nations united to confront Tadodaho again. This time they offered him a special role in the democracy: to preside over all fifty chiefs of the Grand Council Fire. With this generous offer, Tadodaho finally agreed to the Great Peace.

The Great Peacemaker marked the union by digging a hole beneath a great white pine tree. All fifty leaders threw in their weapons of anger, hatred, and revenge—including their hatchets—and buried them. The Great Peacemaker then placed an eagle atop the Great Tree of Peace, so the eagle could use its keen eyesight to warn the Haudenosaunee of any dangers.

To commemorate the peace between the five tribes, Hiawatha made a wampum belt. On Hiawatha's belt, the five tribes are in order. The Seneca are farthest on the left, as they are the keepers of the western door, and the Mohawk farther on the right, as keepers of the eastern door. In the middle is the Great Tree, which represents the Onondaga and the unity among all the tribes.

## GEORGE WASHINGTON'S WAMPUM BELTS

In 1794, a wampum belt was created to symbolize the successful ratification of the Canandaigua Treaty, which restored peace between the American government and the Haudenosaunee. The belt has thirteen figures holding hands, connected to two smaller figures and a longhouse, a traditional Haudenosaunee home. The hands represent the original colonies of America. The two smaller figures represent Tadodaho and George Washington. This wasn't the only wampum belt given to Washington, though. A two-row wampum belt was passed down to Washington from an earlier seventeenth-century peace treaty between Haudenosaunee leaders and Dutch allies, a peace that was then adopted by English and colonial settlers. The two rows represent canoes, a symbol of the two communities living side by side in harmony. This peace treaty, of course, would soon be broken by colonists.

With peace restored, a centralized government was formed: the Grand Council Fire of Haudenosaunee. This council was responsible for establishing the framework of law that governed the people within the Haudenosaunee Confederacy. Because of these oral traditions, we do not know the exact dates of the unification. Some believe it to be as early as 1142, like the Seneca, who according to their oral traditions say the Great Law of Peace was marked by a solar eclipse that happened on August 22, 1142. Others place it later, to the mid-fifteenth century.

Regardless of who you ask, this means the confederacy remains the oldest living participatory democracy on earth. A participatory democracy is one where the citizens have the right to vote and make decisions, just like in the

United States. In short, these nations founded a central multistate government while maintaining their individual tribal governance. Sound familiar? The United States has a federal government and individual state governments for all fifty states. Each state maintains their own local laws, while collectively adhering to federal laws.

Let's take a closer look at how the Haudenosaunee Confederacy operated. To begin with, the Grand Council Fire was made up of fifty chiefs who represented the original five nations (now six). The capital of the confederacy was Onondaga. This is where the chiefs would meet to make important decisions, traditionally around a fire. Here are how decisions in the Grand Council Fire were made:

The Chiefs of the Onondaga Nation serve as the Council's Firekeepers and are responsible for hearing the matters of the Haudenosaunee, who sit between the Elder Brothers and Younger Brothers. The Firekeepers shall then offer propose an issue for discussion. Each issue must be unanimously agreed upon by the Grand Council before it is drawn from the Well.

Once an issue of particular importance is agreed upon for discussion, the Elder Brother Chiefs of the Seneca and Mohawk Nation shall draw the issue from the *Well* and introduce it to the Council. They shall then pass the issue to Younger Brother Chiefs of the Oneida and Cayuga Nation (including the Chiefs of the Tuscarora Nation who speak through the Oneidas in Council).

The Younger Brothers shall then discuss the standing issue. After deliberating upon the standing issue, the Chiefs of the

Younger Brothers will then either support the resolution or ask the Elder Brother Chiefs to reconsider their position with the recommendations of the Younger Brothers in mind. If both sides of the house become of one mind, the Elder Brothers shall then pass the standing issue to the Firekeepers of the Onondaga Nation to further discuss the matter.

After deliberating upon the standing issue, the Firekeepers will then either confirm the resolution or ask the Elder Brothers and Younger Brothers to reconsider their position with the recommendations of the Firekeepers in mind. The Council shall continue to deliberate in this fashion until they come to one mind through consensus building.

—"Grand Council Fire of the Haudenosaunee,"
Kahnawake Branch of the Mohawk Nation, Six Nation
Iroquois Confederacy, http://www.kahnawakelonghouse.com/
index.php?mid=1

Decisions in the Haudenosaunee were and continue to be made through consensus, or a general agreement. This means the majority of people must agree to an issue before enacting it as law. This is the core of their democracy and is also the core of later democracies like the United States of America. In America, the citizens are given the right to participate in decision-making by having the equal right to voice, or cast, their own vote. The Haudenosaunee Constitution also spells out a system of checks and balances. These are measures to ensure that no one tribe has too much power or influence. The US Constitution borrowed a similar measure when it created the judicial (Supreme Court), executive (President), and legislative (Congress) branches of government, which all work together to balance and separate power. Article 1, Section 6, Clause 2 of the US Constitution, also known as the Sinecure Clause (or Ineligibility Clause), restricts members of Congress from holding more than one government office or position (because of conflicts of interest). A similar clause can also be found in the Haudenosaunee Constitution.

But perhaps the most progressive part of the Haudenosaunee Constitution was that it granted political power to women, by allowing them to nominate and impeach (remove) chiefs, as tribal nations within the Haudenosaunee Confederacy were matrilineal.

## WHAT'S THAT PHRASE?

A *matrilineal society* is one where family relations are traced through the mother's bloodline, not the father's. Women hold primary positions of power and are also an intrinsic part of spirituality and creation stories. This resulted in women being the ones at the top making decisions. Matrilineal Indigenous communities believed women had a stronger connection to Mother Earth.

Within tribes, power between the sexes was equal. Clan mothers were in the highest position. They had final say on all decisions and they were the ones in charge of selecting the next leader of the tribe. Equality of the sexes is one element that the Founders most certainly did not adopt. It wasn't until the Nineteenth Amendment was added to the US Constitution in 1920 that women became legally allowed to vote. Native Americans wouldn't have full citizenship and the right to vote until 1924.

The Haudenosaunee Confederacy is in no way the exact model used by the Founders, the men who crafted and framed the US Constitution. But it is impossible to ignore the similarities, especially considering that the Grand Council chiefs were invited to congressional meetings just weeks before the United States declared its independence. In 1988, the US Congress issued a formal resolution to acknowledge their influence.

> Whereas the original framers of the Constitution, including, most notably, George Washington and Benjamin Franklin, are known to have greatly admired the concepts of the Six Nations of the Iroquois Confederacy; Whereas the confederation of the original Thirteen Colonies into one republic was influenced by the political system developed by the Iroquois Confederacy as were many of the democratic principles which were incorporated into the Constitution itself.

Despite this slight recognition from the US government, most contributions from the Haudenosaunee, like most Indigenous tribes, remain uncredited and overlooked by the general public. For instance, consider the Great Seal of the US government: the bald eagle holding an olive branch in one talon and thirteen arrows in the other. In its beak is a scroll with America's motto: *E pluribus unum*. The motto is Latin, and in English means "Out of many, one." This is arguably the most recognizable symbol and one that can be found on all federal buildings and official federal documents. Yet, when comparing this imagery and the symbolism we see in the story of the Great Peacemaker (an eagle atop a tree) and the history surrounding the formation of the Haudenosaunee Confederacy (five tribal nations who came together as one), the resemblance is uncanny.

As you'll learn more throughout this book, much of Native American history has been intentionally left out and overlooked. The story of the Three Sisters, another oral tradition that would inform and sustain white European culture, is up next.

# CHAPTER 3
## THE THREE SISTERS
## AND THE ORIGIN OF MAIZE

*It was said that the earth began when "Sky Woman" who lived in the upper world peered through a hole in the sky and fell through to an endless sea. The animals saw her coming, so they took the soil from the bottom of the sea and spread it onto the back of a giant turtle to provide a safe place for her to land. This "Turtle Island" is now what we call North America. Sky woman had become pregnant before she fell. When she landed, she gave birth to a daughter. When the daughter grew into a young woman, she also became pregnant (by the West wind). She died while giving birth to twin boys. Sky Woman buried her daughter in the "new earth." From her grave grew three sacred plants—corn, beans, and squash. These plants provided food for her sons, and later, for all of humanity. These special gifts ensured the survival of the [Haudenosaunee] people.*

—Northeastern State University, "Three Sisters Legend,"
*https://www.nsuok.edu/heritage/three-sisters-legend.aspx*

And so goes one version of the legend of the Three Sisters, a popular story in Native American folklore tradition. Though the legend varies depending on which Native community you hear it from, the basis of corn, beans, and squash, needing to grow together in order to ensure the best harvest possible remains the same.

## TURTLE ISLAND

Many tribes refer to the entire continent of North America as "Turtle Island." The turtle is an important figure in many different tribes' creation stories as it represents healing, wisdom, protection, and fertility, among other things. Take a look at a map; you might notice that the entire shape of North America is similar to the shape of a giant turtle.

The Three Sisters was an agricultural technique used all across Native American culture from tribes as far west as the Mandan in present-day North Dakota to the Haudenosaunee in the Northeast. The Three Sisters represent corn, beans, and squash. When grown together, the plants help to support one another. Native Americans would bury rotten fish and eels in a mound of soil as fertilizer and then add the corn, beans, and squash seeds, or the Three Sisters. The corn stalk would provide a strong structure for the beans to grow up. The beans would provide nitrogen in the soil, which is essential for corn growth. The squash would grow along the bottom, providing shade to prevent weeds from growing. Today, we recognize this practice as an early iteration of biodynamic farming.

## WHAT'S THAT WORD?

**Biodynamic** is a more ethical and holistic approach to farming. This type of farming relies purely on natural means of production like the rain and the sun and doesn't rely on modern practices like using pesticides. Though popularized by Austrian philosopher Rudolf Steiner in the early 1920s, Native communities had been applying the practice to their food growing and gathering methods for centuries before.

When the first European settlers arrived in North America, they knew nothing of the Three Sisters legend or planting method and struggled to grow crops successfully on land they were unfamiliar with. Instead, they were attempting to grow crops with methods they'd used in Europe and due to the soil being vastly different, their future began to look very grim. Now known as the "Starving Time," more than four-fifths of the five hundred settlers in Jamestown in 1609 were dead by March of 1610. Their lack of agricultural knowledge, low-running supplies, and tense relations with neighboring Native tribes all culminated in widespread settler deaths during those early winters. Eventually, white settlers noticed Native American tribes successfully farming enough crops to feed entire villages. Though tensions still ran high and peace was tenuous—a different reality from the Thanksgiving tales we've been taught—the white settlers were let in on the Three Sisters agricultural technique. The Three Sisters is considered one of the most essential pieces of knowledge gained by Europeans that ensured their survival in the "New World" (as they mistakenly called it) after their fatal first winters.

## THE THANKSGIVING MYTH

Chances are you learned the story of Thanksgiving as local Native Americans in Plymouth welcoming the courageous Pilgrims to a celebratory feast. But in an interview with *Smithsonian Magazine*, David Silverman, the author of *This Land Is Their Land: The Wampanoag*

*Indians, Plymouth Colony, and the Troubled History of Thanksgiving*, had this to say: "The myth is that friendly Indians, unidentified by tribe, welcome the Pilgrims to America, teach them how to live in this new place, sit down to dinner with them and then disappear. They hand off America to white people so they can create a great nation dedicated to liberty, opportunity and Christianity for the rest of the world to profit. That's the story—it's about Native people conceding to colonialism. It's bloodless and in many ways an extension of the ideology of Manifest Destiny.... The Thanksgiving myth doesn't address the deterioration of this relationship culminating in one of the most horrific colonial Indian wars on record, King Philip's War, and also doesn't address Wampanoag survival and adaptation over the centuries, which is why they're still here, despite the odds." Silverman says the retelling of this inaccurate myth is deeply damaging to Wampanoag and other Indigenous communities today.

To this day, Indigenous knowledge has inspired many of America's modern agricultural techniques. At the beginning of the last century, corn farmers experienced soil erosion creating a dust bowl effect as, in many parts of the country, land that was once fertile lost its ability to retain necessary nutrients and moisture. Things took a turn for the better when farmers, taking note of the Three Sisters method, began to introduce the soybean to their land. They quickly noticed that if they rotated their fields between corn and soybeans, the nitrogen in the roots of the soybeans would return the soil to the perfect state for growing corn. This crop rotation technique came directly from the Three Sisters and its use today, just like its use in history, has saved many from starvation.

The Three Sisters are not the only example of Indigenous knowledge being used to change the world of modern agriculture. Much of the food we eat today is genetically modified. You might think of genetically modified organisms, or GMOs, as a fairly modern invention, but the first time in history when humans modified a plant species to better suit their needs was actually accomplished by Indigenous people in central Mexico nearly nine thousand years ago.

This plant was called maize, or what we know today as corn. Over generations, Indigenous people modified the plant by suppressing its branches. This allowed for fewer ears per stalk, but increased the number of kernels per ear.

This modification led to the creation of our modern ear of corn. Using multiple DNA analyses, scientists have found the closest relative to maize in its original region alongside many ancient tools used for grinding maize. That relative of maize was a tall grass with kernels covered in a hard case. Today, maize is grown globally; in fact, between 2019 and 2020, an estimated 1,108 million tonnes were produced. The United States is the world's largest corn producer, with over eighty million acres devoted to the cultivation of this crop. None of this would have been possible without the ingenuity of Indigenous people almost ten thousand years earlier. That ancient story is up next.

# CHAPTER 4
## CAHOKIA: AN ANCIENT CITY

In school, you've probably learned about the Aztec, Inca, and Maya civilizations. But did you ever learn about Cahokia? Have you ever heard of it? American school children are often taught that Christopher Columbus discovered America, and that European settlers were the first people to ever civilize the New World. That, as we've already discussed, is a myth. Cahokia offers an excellent lens through which we can see a different story emerge, a complex and sophisticated world that existed long before the Europeans ever showed up.

With the arrival of Christopher Columbus in the Caribbean in 1492, we read in his diaries the first of many times Indigenous people are referred to as primitive and less advanced than Europeans. For hundreds of years, Europeans adopted this mindset, enslaving, murdering, and attempting to "civilize" and erase Indigenous people across the Americas. This belief in cultural superiority was supported by the Catholic church in Europe with what was called the Doctrine of Discovery. Pope Alexander VI even issued Columbus his Doctrine of Discovery in 1493, declaring that any land he "discovered" would belong to Spain. In other words, Spain, with the help of the powerful Catholic church, stole the land from the people already living there. This is the first documented theft of Indigenous land in the Americas.

## WHAT'S THAT PHRASE?

*Cultural superiority*, or *cultural imperialism*, is when one culture decides it's better than another and acts on that belief. You may have seen a microcosm of this in your own life: One group of kids thinks they're better than everyone else and tries to rule the school. But when one powerful culture decides it's better, more sophisticated, more civilized than a native culture, then invades it and imposes its values, beliefs, and practices on that culture, it can have a devastating effect on the native population.

## HISTORY RECAP

The **Doctrine of Discovery** was central to the Spanish conquest of the New World. It stated that any land not already inhabited by Christians was available to be "discovered" and claimed. Pope Alexander VI declared that "the Catholic faith and the Christian religion be exalted and be everywhere increased and spread, that the health of souls be cared for and that barbarous nations be overthrown and brought to the faith itself." This doctrine, which basically called colonization a God-given right, formed the justification of the United States' western expansion. In the 1823 case *Johnson v. M'Intosh*, Supreme Court Chief Justice John Marshall's opinion was that European nations had the absolute right to New World lands. Which meant Native Americans had no rights to them.

There are many arguments to be made against this European belief in cultural superiority over Indigenous people in the Americas, but one major one stands out: a massive archaeological discovery, in what is modern-day Illinois, that throws a wrench in the lie that civilization can be defined by European standards. The discovery is of the ancient city of

Cahokia, which existed from about 1050 to 1400 CE. It was the largest pre-Columbian settlement north of Mexico.

## HISTORY RECAP: PRE-COLUMBIAN PERIOD

At its peak, Cahokia was the same size as London at the time! It was a thriving city filled with huge mounds and vast open plazas and houses. The city had a population of over ten thousand and another twenty to thirty thousand people living in the city's suburbs. In total, it covered about six square miles. It was structured very much the way we live now, with the city at its center, surrounded by smaller villages, and farmland outside those villages.

Lori Belknap, the superintendent of the Cahokia Mounds State Historic Site, told True History that what really distinguishes the site are its eighty earthen mounds. (There were once 120 mounds at Cahokia.) They have different shapes and purposes, and some are huge. Picture a grass-covered ancient pyramid. Visitors to Cahokia can climb Monks Mound, which is the largest at one hundred feet tall. Belknap says they know through years of archaeological digs and other research that the mounds were engineering feats, built with hoes, dirt, and forty-pound baskets used to deliver the dirt to the mounds.

Many Europeans thought that Indigenous people had no hierarchy or structured government. But in some of the mounds, archaeologists made discoveries that suggest the possibility of Cahokian royalty. Mound 72 was a burial place for a very important person: the "Birdman." Belknap says they know that because he was buried with a lot of exotic items, things of high value. "He was laid out on a cape shaped like a raptor bird that was made of tens of thousands of marine shell beads. Each bead was handcrafted." The beads came from the Atlantic or Gulf Coast, so someone had to travel a long way to get them there.

Archaeologists and researchers have also uncovered evidence that Cahokia was a planned city with avenues and designated community zones. Belknap says the city was shaped like a diamond, with other organizational patterns within. This dispels the notion that Indigenous people were less advanced than Europeans in the construction and operation of their civilizations.

Belknap says visiting Cahokia also helps dispel some other common stereotypes (see page 64 for a definition) perpetuated in film and TV, and even in classrooms. The term *hunter-gatherers* is often used as a blanket description for Indigenous people, which supports this false notion of European superiority. But archaeologists discovered advanced agricultural techniques utilized by the Mississippians who lived in Cahokia. In digs of farmsteads surrounding the city itself, there is concrete evidence of "adaptive strategy," which shows their agricultural strategies evolved with the explosion of the population.

"When Mississippian culture started developing, one of the hallmarks of it was that they practiced large-scale agriculture," says Belknap, "which allowed people to stay in one location and build these bigger cities versus earlier periods where they were nomadic and living in smaller groups. And we see that organization happening around the globe at the same time."

## WHAT'S THAT WORD?

**Mississippians** is the name given to multiple Native American communities that populated the Midwest and the eastern and southeastern regions of what is now the United States from 800 CE to 1600 CE. (CE, or Common

Era, is the secular, or nonreligious, version of AD, which means "in the year of the Lord.") The Mississippians controlled trade along the Mississippi River. The word *Mississippi* comes from the Ojibwe word *Misi-Ziibi*, meaning "Great River." The Mississippi River begins in North Minnesota, the traditional homelands of the Anishinaabe (Ojibwe). These cities and their satellite villages were linked together by trading networks, with Cahokia being the largest, or the capital. Belknap says it was a very complex civilization and that many of these communities shared similar lifestyles with those who lived in Cahokia. Many remnants of this ancient civilization exist in modern tribal groups who live close to the river. The use of a major waterway might explain the far-reaching influence of Cahokian culture on these different tribal groups.

This has also led many researchers to believe Cahokia had a central government that could direct labor where it saw fit and stockpile resources for state-sponsored development projects. People previously believed these state governments only existed in ancient times in Mesopotamia, Mexico, Peru, and China.

Tribes such as the Osage and Pawnee, who some researchers believe to be the modern descendants of Cahokians, had a major impact on European explorers. As Europeans attempted to cross these central territories of what we now know as the United States, they were met by fierce nations. Some historians attribute the strength of these nations to Cahokia's previous dominance in the region.

What happened to Cahokia? Nobody knows for certain. Unlike Pompeii, which was buried under lava when Mount Vesuvius erupted, there is no one cataclysmic event that dissolved Cahokia. Belknap says it's likely that a number of factors contributed to its decline over a period of years, rather than all at once. She says they probably began to run out of resources, and there could have been a few years of poor leadership. But they have yet to find any real evidence of what caused people to leave.

Unfortunately, for many years, the site of Cahokia was disregarded as simply natural formations of the earth. There were a number of influential people who argued that the mounds could not have been made by Indigenous people. And so highways, housing subdivisions, and businesses were built on the site, destroying some of its structures and with it, valuable history. In the field of anthropology and archaeology, this destruction of an ancient archaeological site is directly tied to the long-held belief in the superiority of European civilizations over Indigenous cultures. Despite the widespread destruction of the site, Cahokia remains an extremely important testament to the advanced ability and knowledge base of the Indigenous people of North America. And today, not only is it a US National Historic Landmark, but it is also a UNESCO World Heritage site.

## WHAT DOES *THAT* MEAN?

A **UNESCO World Heritage site** is a landmark that has legal protection under a convention overseen by an international body, the United Nations Educational, Scientific, and Cultural Organization. There are currently 1,154 sites in 167 countries.

Belknap explains why it's vital to preserve Cahokia: "It's important to let people know that there was a huge city with a huge sphere of influence—this sphere of influence was basically the entire Midwest and all the way to Florida. For Americans to be able to identify with our history, I think it's important to understand this level of our history and what was here one thousand years ago."

Many Indigenous people today struggle with the fact that history and the American education system have often omitted our stories and perspectives from books and research. But our knowledge base is tens of thousands of years rich in the experience of living on this land, passed down from generation to generation.

There is power in the past. That story is up next.

## LET'S TALK ABOUT IT

* Why do you think that for so long archaeologists and historians could not believe that Indigenous people created the mounds at Cahokia?

* Has learning about Cahokia changed your views of Indigenous history?

# CHAPTER 5
## POWER IN THE PAST

*There is power in the past. What we have for power in the present comes from what's written about the past. And archaeologists are very aware of that, that the longer a people have been in an area, the stronger their claims to be Indigenous to that area, their claims to land, to artifacts in that land, to anything that's in the land, to their identity, to their history. It's very empowering for Indigenous people to reclaim their history and teach others about it.*
—Dr. Paulette Steeves, Indigenous archaeologist (Cree-Metis)

How long have Indigenous people been in the Americas? You might think that is a simple question. But there is currently no definitive answer, and archaeologists and historians are not all in agreement on this subject.

Indigenous communities know that Native Americans have lived on the continent now called North America for tens of thousands of years. But for a long time, most archaeologists subscribed to the Bering Strait and Clovis First theories, which state that tool-using humans migrated from Siberia to Alaska via a land bridge around thirteen thousand years ago. The Bering Strait Theory was often taught to American school children. And until the late twentieth century, many archaeologists were convinced that the Clovis, named for Clovis, New Mexico, were the first Indigenous people in the Americas. More recently, various archaeological digs—in Oregon, Idaho, and other locations in North America—squashed that theory and put humans in the Americas as many as sixteen thousand years ago.

A discovery announced in 2021 confirmed what many Indigenous people already believed: that we have been in the Americas even longer than that. Thousands of ancient footprints were found preserved in the ground across the White Sands National Park in New Mexico dating back twenty-three thousand years ago, to the Ice Age. There are also footprints left by animals such as mammoths, camels, wolves, and giant sloths.

## HOW'D THEY DO THAT?

The archaeologists working at the White Sands site collected ancient seeds of ditch grass from between the toes of the footprints and brought them to a lab and measured the carbon in them. Their tests found that the seeds had grown thousands of years before the end of the last ice age. The oldest human and mammoth footprints at the site were located near seeds that are roughly 22,800 years old. These numbers might sound astounding, but there are Indigenous scholars who believe Indigenous people have been here much longer than that. There is a common saying among Native people: "We have been here since time immemorial," meaning ancient beyond memory or record.

Dr. Paulette Steeves, a Canada Research Chair at Algoma University, argues that Indigenous people have been in the Americas at least 130,000 years! Steeves has been collecting data on Pleistocene Indigenous sites in the Americas and now counts some four hundred sites that are over 11,000 years old, the oldest ones 200,000 years. There's a cave area in New Mexico that dates to 50,000 years ago, a site in Georgia of similar age, one in Brazil, and multiple sites in California.

## WHAT'S THAT PHRASE?

The **Pleistocene** is the geological period that lasted from about 2,580,000 years ago to 11,700 years ago.

But Steeves blames a history of colonizer racism for the inability of most scientists to accept that Indigenous people have been in the Americas much longer than they claim.

> If you look at the Americas overall, you have a nation state built on stolen land, and to steal the land, you need to erase the identities of the people that you stole it from. You need to make it okay to take it. So early on in archaeology, we were called savages. We were more linked to nature than culture. It's taken since the early 1900s for archaeologists to admit that yes, we did build the mounds; yes, we did have great culture; yes, we did have intellect and medicine and science.

Even today, there is still disagreement about how long Indigenous people have been in North and South America, and how they got there. Steeves argues that one of the problems with modern archaeology is that it often refuses to go directly to an important source: the Indigenous people whose ancestors have told them the stories of their people through oral traditions.

You may remember we talked about oral traditions in

earlier chapters. Oral traditions are the firsthand observations passed down verbally from one generation to the next, and every Indigenous community has its own individual history. Oral traditions can describe migration patterns; illuminate the cultural attributes, knowledge, and accomplishments of a community; and describe the science, medicine, and religion practiced by a certain people. And they can help tell us how long Indigenous people have been in certain places.

For example, Steeves says that some people have oral traditions of mammoths and mastodons, animals that have been extinct for at least ten thousand years. She says the Osage people have an oral tradition about a battle between mammoths and mastodons.

> The Osage people went back to that battle site (on the Pomme de Terre River in what is now Missouri), and they burned a lot of the mammoths and mastodons to respect them, and then they had a ceremony every year after that to honor the spirit of those animals. So, what did archaeologists later find at that site? They found a huge bunch of burned mammoth and mastodon remains and stone tools.

Stories like this one and rock drawings of other animals that are extinct can help an archaeologist understand how long Indigenous people have been in a particular place. (There are thousands of rock art sites in both North and South America.)

According to Steeves, the oral traditions of people's time and place on the land are actual historical accounts that come from firsthand knowledge and experience. But Steeves says most non-Indigenous archaeologists have long dismissed oral traditions as unscientific because they can't be quantified and measured in the same way that archaeological finds can be.

## COOL CAREER: ARCHAEOLOGIST

We asked Paulette Steeves what being an archaeologist is like. Here's what she told us: "As a Canada Research Chair and archaeologist, my job entails doing research on archaeological sites. As an undergraduate, I carried out DNA analysis that helped an Indigenous community reclaim five hundred sets of ancestors' remains for burial from museums that were refusing to return them, even though it was required by law. It was then I realized that being an archaeologist offered many ways that I could support Indigenous communities. And when I learned that the Clovis First hypothesis of people first coming here twelve hundred years ago wasn't based on fact but on conjecture, I realized there was a lot of hypocrisy and racism in how the field of American archaeology has written and understood Indigenous history. So my job is to research that, to show that these theories are wrong, and that there is evidence of people being on the land much earlier."

When archaeologists work hand-in-hand with oral traditions, they can help Indigenous people reclaim their history. And that work can also educate the general population about Indigenous life in the Americas.

Steeves says if young people want to learn more about this topic or other areas of Indigenous history, it's important to consider their sources.

> They need to think about who wrote the story. There's always more than one story. And they need to realize what you see is a bunch of European people writing Indigenous history without having any understanding of those Indigenous people. So they need to think critically when they're reading something, about who wrote this and how did they frame it?

Mainstream media like newspapers often ignore, whether intentionally or not, Indigenous perspectives and voices when writing history.

Steeves says to look for books written by Indigenous authors because there are plenty (visit the Selected Bibliography on page 176 for suggestions). The Bering Strait and Clovis

First theories are just two of the many myths surrounding Indigenous origins that have been debunked. A look at other myths about Indigenous culture is up next.

## LET'S TALK ABOUT IT

* Do you think it's important to read source material on Indigenous history written by Indigenous authors? Why or why not?

# PART 2: MYTHS

# CHAPTER 6
## MYTHS, STEREOTYPES, AND TROPES ABOUT INDIGENOUS PEOPLE

You may have heard the term "fake news" pop up a lot in the news recently. Many politicians and talk show hosts have used the term to discredit the media, press, or an evolving news story. The term is a way for someone to tell another person that they believe what they are saying is wrong—or fake. And while the term might seem like a new concept, it's actually been around for centuries (just called a variety of other names). But figuring out what is real news versus fake news isn't such an easy task.

That's because throughout history, stories and events are often written by a person or group of people with a particular agenda, meaning that the writer produces a story with a desired outcome in mind. To carry out that agenda, the writer often only gives certain details of a story while leaving out other details entirely.

For example, you probably heard the old singsong saying, "In 1492, Columbus sailed the ocean blue," right? That's not an inaccurate statement: Christopher Columbus did, in fact, commission a fleet of ships from Spain in 1492, looking for a new trade route from Europe to India. Here's where the history becomes troublesome and enters the realm of so-called fake news.

When their ships made landfall in October of 1492, Columbus assumed he was in the Indies, when he was on one of the Bahamian islands. Here, Columbus was greeted by the Arawak, a group of Indigenous people from present-day South America and the Caribbean. Thinking he was in the Indies, Columbus called them *los Indios*, meaning "the Indians." We know this because he recorded it in his journal.

> They willingly traded everything they owned . . . They were well-built, with good bodies and handsome features . . . They do not bear arms, and do not know them, for I showed them a sword, they took it by the edge and cut themselves out of ignorance. They have no iron . . . They would make fine servants . . . With fifty men we could subjugate them all and make them do whatever we want.

Now, the question arises: Can you discover a land that is already inhabited? Most would readily agree that no, you cannot. Yet that flawed logic hasn't stopped this myth from prevailing as it serves as a positive origin story for the United States—a story in which Columbus is the hero brave enough to chart the unknown seas to ultimately discover the New World.

But when you consider that Columbus had an agreement with Ferdinand and Isabella, the monarchs of Spain who financed his voyage, that he could keep 10 percent of the riches he found, along with a noble title and governorship of any lands he should encounter, we begin to see a clearer agenda that, unsurprisingly, again comes down to land ownership.

So, not only is it an incorrect statement to say Columbus "discovered" America, but as we'll discuss next, the messaging of false claims and other myths like this are all part of a larger coordinated effort—or an agenda—to overwrite and erase Indigenous history.

The claim of Columbus's discovery of America is just one example in the very long list of myths that underscore Indigenous history—a history that long precedes Columbus.

A more recent example on that same list can be seen in the Disney movie *Pocahontas*. While the movie was a box office success, bringing in $346 million, it certainly could be cast as "fake news" as the Hollywood story relies on historical inaccuracies, harmful racial stereotypes, and other false tropes about Native Americans.

## WHAT'S THAT WORD?

A **stereotype** is an oversimplified idea or image of a person or group, usually based on class, religion, gender, or other cultural habits.

A **trope** is an idea, image, or theme that occurs across media, like the "mad scientist" in film, for instance.

Here are some other myths, stereotypes, and tropes that need clarification.

### II. Native Americans Did Not
### Have an Uncivilized Culture

Just two hundred years after Columbus's arrival in the Americas, European colonial settlers like John Smith (more on him later) began arriving along the eastern coast of what is now the United States. As you may have already learned, colonial settlers left their homeland of England, many escaping religious persecution, like the Pilgrims who settled in Plymouth, Massachusetts, in the early 1600s. Still, much of the land was occupied by Natives, who had been living there for generations. This was a problem. Or was it?

In an exclusive interview with True History, Michael Witgen, who is a professor in the Department of History at Columbia University and a citizen of the Red Cliff Band of Lake Superior Ojibwe, had this to say:

> Most European powers claim their territory by right of discovery, which is an archaic international law concept that imagines North America as not the property or dominion of any particular people. It imagines that Native people have no more right to their territory than animals that live on that territory because they haven't created regimes and governments that are recognizable as civilized in Europe. So, once you frame the continent that way as unsettled, there's no real future for Native people.

In other words, by the logic of the English colonists, the Native Americans could not own the land because in their eyes they were equivalent to "animals" who hadn't established territorial borders or a proper government as they had done in Europe. This, as we have learned in Chapter 1, is false. But by believing in this "archaic natural law" as Witgen suggests, the Europeans practicing settler colonialism viewed the land as their own, since, the way they saw it, it was unsettled.

## WHAT DOES *THAT* MEAN?

**Settler colonialism** is a form of colonialism in which an invading settler society seeks to replace the Indigenous (original) population of a territory, often through violence and domination.

This worldview would become a collective mantra for early settlers and colonial leaders, known as "manifest destiny," the belief that expansion throughout the United States was not only justified but inevitable. The term was coined in 1845 and many of its advocates believed that they were destined by God to spread democracy across the country.

### III. Native Americans Are Not a People of the Past

Here's a quick exercise: Google "Native Americans" and see what images pop up first. Chances are you won't find many images of doctors, university professors, professional artists, or any other modern Native American people. Why is that? That's because many Americans today, for a number of reasons, believe we are simply a people of the past to be read about in history books. That couldn't be further from the truth.

Each semester, Professor Witgen, who teaches a survey history of Native North America at Columbia University, attempts to educate his students on the true history of Indigenous people. And one of the most prevailing tropes that Witgen addresses is that Native Americans somehow knew their extinction was imminent as European settlers colonized their land and way of life. Witgen says:

> What I want to preserve is how—in a given moment of time—Native people weren't thinking they were on their way out. They weren't imagining that their future had been foreclosed and that it was nothing but demise and disintegration in the future. That's super important because so much of the history we get is framed that way because so much of the European project is bringing civilization to a continent that hasn't been settled. A way to imagine a Native presence as being part of this archaic past that can only go away as this future, represented by civilization in Europe arrives. Throughout all Native history, Native people are trying to imagine a future for themselves even when increasingly powerful outside forces like colonial empires [arrive]. It's a constant trope that shows up in settler narratives that are written with an eye toward producing an outcome that results in the [extinction] of Indian civilization.

Again, here we have yet another example of a clear agenda in the making—one that overrides and excludes the perspective of Native Americans while presenting the colonial settlers as the knights in shining armor rescuing Natives from their uncivilized way of life. With this mindset, European settlers believe they have every right to claim the land as their own. But this simply isn't the case. Witgen continues:

> Anglo [English] settlement in North America is framed around this idea of Natural Law, which allows Great Britain to claim North America as a possession of the king by the right of discovery. And it imagines that North America is a world that hasn't been civilized, that native people [live in a community] with no private property they hadn't progressed out of. This kind of ideology imagines a framework of settlement as bringing civilization to a world that hasn't been settled—civilization to a world that is uncivilized. So, if you are framing it way, then there is no future for Native people because they represent this sort of primal past.

Unfortunately, as you likely saw from that Google search, the framework and mindset of the early colonial settlers continues to serve as the foundation for this popular trope to this very day.

## IV. The Myth of Incompetency

Another myth that has prevailed since 1626 is that the Lenape Indians sold the island of Manhattan to the Dutch for a small amount of trinkets. While that part is, in fact, true, there is much more to this story to place this purchase into historical context. First, here is a translation (from Dutch) of the letter from Peter Schaghen, a representative of the West India Company:

*High and Mighty Lords,*

*Yesterday the ship the Arms of Amsterdam arrived here. It sailed from New Netherland out of the River Mauritius on the 23d of September. They report that our people are in good spirit and live in peace. The women also have borne some children there. They have purchased the Island Manhattes from the Indians for the value of 60 guilders. It is 11,000 morgens in size [about 22,000 acres].*

*In Amsterdam, the 5th of November anno 1626.*
*Your High and Mightinesses' obedient, P. Schaghen Your High and Mightinesses' obedient, P. Schaghen*

As you can read from Schaghen's letter, the Lenape did sell present-day Manhattan to the Dutch for sixty guilders, which was the Dutch currency from the fifteenth century until it was eventually replaced by the Euro in 2002. But, as Professor Witgen notes, there's a lot more to consider to this purchase.

Similar to the way Columbus described the Arawak as "ignorant" people, this myth builds on a common theme of storytelling: casting the Natives as unintelligent people while setting up the colonists as their intellectual superiors, who have every right to claim the land as their own to establish a civilized culture. There is perhaps no clearer example of this mythology at play than with the story of Pocahontas.

## V. The Story of Pocahontas: A Mythology of Transfer

Chances are you've heard, read, or seen a version of Pocahontas's tale. In 1995, Disney released an animated version of the story about a young Powhatan woman's romantic encounter with John Smith, an English colonial leader who helped found the colony of Virginia in the early 1600s. Disney's version, like so many others, greatly embellishes the truth and distorts the relationship between Pocahontas and John Smith into a romantic one to fit a happy Hollywood ending—one that ignores the brutal reality of colonization. By all accurate accounts, even Smith's own, Pocahontas would have only been around ten years old when she encountered the English colonial solider Smith, who was twenty-seven.

Witgen calls the story of Pocahontas a "mythology of transfer." Witgen says that it is "meant to give legitimacy to English appropriation of native territory and create characters—like Pocahontas—who can be adopted by the Europeans for positive storytelling. She is a signifier of a mythological peaceful welcome to the New World—a much different image than the reality of people who are being conquered, killed, and displaced."

In response to the 1995 film, lifelong Indigenous activist and historian Chief Roy Crazy Horse of the Powhatan Renape Nation challenged Disney, which claimed its film was "responsible, accurate, and respectful."

We of the Powhatan Nation disagree. The film distorts history beyond recognition. Our offers to assist Disney with cultural and historical accuracy were rejected. Our efforts urging him [Disney] to reconsider his misguided mission were spurred.

"Pocahontas" was a nickname, meaning "the naughty one" or "spoiled child." Her real name was Matoaka. The legend is that she saved a heroic John Smith from being clubbed to death by her father in 1607—she would have been about ten or eleven at the time. The truth is that Smith's fellow colonists described him as an abrasive, ambitious, self-promoting mercenary soldier.

Of all of Powhatan's children, only "Pocahontas" is known, primarily because she became the hero of Euro-Americans as the "good Indian," one who saved the life of a white man. Not only is the "good Indian/bad Indian theme" inevitably given new life by Disney, but the history, as recorded by the English themselves, is badly falsified in the name of "entertainment."

The truth of the matter is that the first time John Smith told the story about this rescue was seventeen years after it happened, and it was but one of three reported by the pretentious Smith that he was saved from death by a prominent woman.

Yet in an account Smith wrote after his winter stay with Powhatan's people, he never mentioned such an incident. In fact, the starving adventurer reported he had been kept comfortable and treated in a friendly fashion as an honored guest of Powhatan and Powhatan's brothers. Most scholars think the "Pocahontas incident" would have been highly unlikely, especially since it was part of a longer account used as justification to wage war on Powhatan's nation.

Euro-Americans must ask themselves why it has been so important to elevate Smith's fibbing to status as a national myth worthy of being recycled again by Disney. Disney even improves upon it by changing Pocahontas from a little girl into a young woman.

The true Pocahontas story has a sad ending. In 1612, at the age of seventeen, Pocahontas was treacherously taken prisoner by the English while she was on a social visit, and was held hostage at Jamestown for over a year.

You may be reading this and thinking, *Well, it's only a movie for children.* But that is exactly why it is capable of even more damage. The movie targets young, impressionable kids and teaches them an inaccurate, exaggerated story of a romantic encounter, which will serve as the foundation for their framing of history. And by manipulating the facts of history to fit within the confines of a Hollywood movie, filmmakers are part of this larger agenda to erase Native history and culture by not only glossing over the truth of genocide but making heroes out of people like John Smith.

## VI. Being Native American Is Not One-Size-Fits-All. And We're Not How Hollywood Depicts Us.

Beginning in the late 1930s, Hollywood began producing blockbuster westerns like *Stagecoach*, *Red River*, and *The Searchers*. In these films, a common trope is the clash between two cultures: one "civilized" and one "uncivilized." In this struggle between cowboys and "Indians," Native Americans are almost exclusively depicted as primitive beings and are almost always deemed the enemy and the bad guys, whom the cowboys must protect their fellow people from. And to add insult to injury, Native Americans rarely, if ever, play the roles of Native Americans depicted on screen.

In the early years of westerns, Rock Hudson, a white actor, played a Native in *Winchester '73*. In the 1950 film, Hudson wore face paint and feathered pigtails. Ten years later, in 1960, Audrey Hepburn played a young Native in *The Unforgiven*, who is assimilated into a white family. The film perpetuates several tropes, portraying Natives as unintelligent people ashamed of their own culture. And if you think that these tropes fizzled out once westerns declined in popularity in the late 1960s, well, you'd be wrong. In 2013, Johnny Depp joined the growing list of non-Natives playing Natives when he wore "red face" for his role as Tonto in *The Lone Ranger*. This practice allows filmmakers to exploit and profit off Indigenous culture without allowing Natives to represent themselves on screen. Depp claimed that his role as Tonto was a "salute" to Natives.

These Hollywood tropes are yet another way in which storytellers attempt to degrade our identity by casting all Natives as a one-size-fits-all model. In reality, there are 567 federally recognized Indian nations across the United States. And there are 167 Indigenous languages spoken in the United States. Indigenous Americans are ordinary people contributing to every part of mainstream American society like any other group of people. And while doing so, they maintain their unique traditional culture, knowledge, and language.

Despite this coordinated effort to erase our identity on screen, Indigenous Americans continue to make strides for accurate representation of Natives in television and film. Take filmmaker Sterlin Harjo, for instance. Harjo is a member of the Seminole Nation of Oklahoma and the director of *Reservation Dogs,* a comedy series about Indigenous teens dreaming of life outside of Oklahoma. The show was created by an almost entirely Indigenous crew and writers and features Indigenous actors. Harjo's goal with the series, like all his films, is to 'humanize' the Native experience. "It's not up to Hollywood to change Native representation in the media," Harjo says. "They have failed at it for decades. It's up to us—artists, filmmakers, storytellers, and activists. That power is ours alone."

## VII. Native Americans in Battle

Films, books, and other media resources have traditionally promoted the trope that depicts Native Americans as the savage perpetrators of violence against white Americans, raiding wagon trains of settlers moving west and brutally killing men, women, and children. The reality is these instances were rare. If you think about the history of Hollywood's portrayal of Native Americans in westerns, for example, you can imagine how generations of Americans came to picture Indigenous people as vicious warriors, always antagonizing the settlers, portrayed as innocent victims.

In reality, Indigenous people often fought alongside their European allies, and proved to be invaluable assets to those troops and causes. In the eighteenth century, Colonel James Smith wrote extensively about the Native American warfare tactics he had observed while a captive of the Lenape and Mohawk tribes. He created a comprehensive list of battles in which Native Americans had overrun or equaled European forces with very few losses of their own. He said Native American war tactics were far superior to those utilized by the Europeans because of their ability to work together and move into battle unencumbered. The sophisticated use of communication techniques such as hand signals, bird calls, and mirror flashes proved to be devastating to the enemy. Many of these Native American tactics are still used by the army rangers and other special forces of the US military to this day.

During the French and Indian War, which was a part of the world-wide Seven Years' War, the Haudenosaunee Confederacy allied with the British against the French and a number of other Native American tribes. George Washington was a young military commander during the war, and after, he used many of the battlefield tactics he learned from his

Haudenosaunee allies to win the Revolutionary War, like the reliance on militia forces. These smaller militias would never attack the British head-on, but rather would raid military supply routes and rely heavily on tracking their enemy before an ambush attack.

## HISTORY RECAP: THE FRENCH AND INDIAN WAR (1754–1763)

This was actually a war between the French and their Native American allies (led by the Delaware and Shawnee peoples) on one side, and the British and the Haudenosaunee Confederacy on the other. As more British settlers arrived in the United States, there was a push for westward expansion. At the time, most of North America was controlled by the French and Native Americans. At the beginning of the war, the French and their Native allies dominated, in large part because of their superior alliance. The territory of the upper Ohio River Valley was disputed at the time. Under the leadership of a young General George Washington, the British tried to kick out the French at that location, but were outnumbered and defeated. The British decided to sink a great deal of money into the war effort and strengthened their alliance with the Haudenosaunee Confederacy, which was instrumental in helping the British gain the upper hand. The result: The British eventually won the war, and the Treaty of Paris was signed in 1763, pushing the French out of North America. It's also important to note that in the years leading up to the war, French Catholic missionaries had been successful in converting many Haudenosaunee to Catholicism. In the 1670s, a Haudenosaunee chief had successfully negotiated with both the English and French to ensure his people's interests. Throughout history, we see Haudenosaunee tribes on both sides of conflicts.

Native American warriors went on to fight in every major conflict in US history, including the Revolutionary War and World Wars I and II. By the end of the Civil War, General Ulysses S. Grant's lifelong friend was a Native American man, a Seneca brigadier general named Ely S. Parker, who wrote the final draft for the terms of surrender of the Confederacy, officially ending America's bloodiest conflict. And in World War II, Native American "Code Talkers" were essential in defeating the axis powers.

"Code Talkers" refers to the military radio communication

codes spoken in Native American languages between two Native radio operators, which would then be deciphered on either end of the line and relayed to their respective commanders. The use of the technique proved to be extremely successful in foiling German wiretaps on allied lines of communication throughout WWII.

One of the great ironies of the US military's utilization of Native American languages was the recruitment of Code Talkers directly from boarding schools. These were the very same boarding schools whose main goal was to exterminate all Native languages. (For more information on boarding schools, see page 121.) Let that sink in for a moment.

In the Pacific during WWII, over four hundred Navajos served as Code Talkers. Many faced extreme danger daily, not only from the enemy but also from their fellow American soldiers who would sometimes mistake Code Talkers for Japanese infiltrators. Navajo wasn't the only language utilized. There were codes made from Anishinaabemowin (Ojibwe), Assiniboine, Cherokee, Cheyenne, Chippewa, Choctaw, Comanche, Cree, Crow, Hopi, Kiowa, Menominee, Meskwaki-Sauk, Mohawk, Muscogee, Osage, Pawnee, and Sioux.

## VIII. Sports Mascots "Honor" Native Americans

Following the playbook of actor Johnny Depp and his "salute" to Natives, longtime National Football League (NFL) team owner Dan Snyder claimed that his team's former name, the Washington Redskins, was "honoring Native Americans." Snyder, who once famously touted that he would never change his team's name, finally retired the name in 2020 after mounting public pressure. It took decades of protesting from Native American organizers, beginning in 1967 and capping off with the protests of 2020.

The word *redskin* is a direct reference to Native Americans, and despite Snyder's claims, it is not a good or honorable reference. Since the word's beginnings, dating back to the early 1800s, it has been used disparagingly against Indigenous people. The reality is, like the "redskin scalps" many white settlers made their fortunes collecting, the Washington Redskins' fight to preserve their name and mascot came down to money, not the rights of human beings. In 2020, before their name change, the Washington Redskins franchise had the eighth most profitable merchandising business in the entire NFL.

But the Redskins weren't the only American athletic

franchise to use negative stereotypes about Native Americans to promote their teams and money-making franchises. In Major League Baseball (MLB), the Atlanta Braves are still using a tomahawk as their logo. Braves fans can be seen doing the "tomahawk chop," raising and lowering their hands in a chopping motion—yet another inaccurate and disparaging trope. The "chop" came under scrutiny in the 2019 National League Division series between the Atlanta Braves and the St. Louis Cardinals, when Ryan Helsley, a Cardinal relief pitcher and a member of the Cherokee Nation, stated that the "tomahawk chop" was disrespectful.

> I think it's a misrepresentation of the Cherokee people or Native Americans in general. Just depicts them in this kind of caveman-type people way, who aren't intellectual. They are a lot more than that. It's not me being offended by the whole mascot thing. It's not. It's about the misconception of us, the Native Americans, and it devalues us and how we're perceived.

In 2021, when the Braves played in the World Series, former president Trump attended game four where he, too, joined fans in doing the tomahawk chop.

And while the Braves continue to maintain their name, the Cleveland Indians (MLB), after years of similar controversy and repeated calls from activists to retire the name, did so in the midst of the 2021 season. They are now known as the Cleveland Guardians. Like the Braves, the Kansas City Chiefs (NFL), Chicago Blackhawks (NHL), and Florida State Seminoles (NCAA) continue to profit off Indigenous communities.

When Americans and non-Americans debate the use of Native American names and stereotypes in professional and college sports, there is something much bigger at stake—more than just a name. It is a recognition of centuries of American demonization of Indigenous people. And when sports franchises change a team's name to something that is not offensive, they are taking a step in the right direction. It is one small step in correcting a series of wrongs that have been perpetrated against Native American people for centuries—some of which have been acknowledged and some of which have not.

## LET'S TALK ABOUT IT

* Do you think that the professional sports teams who use Native American names should retire their names?

# PART 3: ERASURE

# CHAPTER 7
## DISEASE, WAR, AND MASS MURDER

You have lived through an unusual time in modern history: the COVID-19 pandemic. It has been difficult for all and devastating for many families. Native Americans have been disproportionately hard-hit by the pandemic, with higher rates of infection, hospitalization, and death than white Americans.

As tragic as it has been for people all over the world, imagine if there were no vaccines, no treatments, no modern hospitals. Imagine if you were an Indigenous person, living on land being colonized by European settlers, and suddenly a strange disease struck your people. You'd never seen this disease before because it didn't exist in your society until the Europeans arrived in North America. It is ugly, it spreads like wildfire, and it is deadly. The disease is smallpox.

## HISTORY RECAP: SMALLPOX

We are lucky that smallpox can be put in a history recap category because it was eradicated by the 1980s. Hopefully, someday we'll say the same for COVID-19. Like COVID, smallpox can produce fever, body aches, severe fatigue, and back pain. A particular marker of smallpox is that it can produce a severe rash all over the body, which can leave scars. And in some cases, it has caused blindness.

Smallpox isn't the only viral menace the settler colonists brought with them. Chicken pox, bubonic plague, cholera, influenza, and measles are some of the other infectious diseases that made their way to North America for the first time with the arrival of the Europeans. Because these illnesses were new to the Indigenous population, they had no natural immunities to them. But smallpox was the deadliest. Smallpox was unknown in this part of the world until it first appeared in Hispaniola in 1507; Hernán Cortés's people brought it to Mesoamerica in 1520. And then in the seventeenth century, the Puritans brought it to the North American colonies. There would be multiple outbreaks for a few hundred years, and it ultimately killed hundreds of millions of people.

## HISTORY RECAP

**Hernán Cortés** (1485–1547) was a vicious Spanish conquistador (explorer and invader) who was an early colonizer of the Americas. Known for his brutality, he led an expedition that caused the fall of the Aztec empire and conquered much of what is now Mexico.

## WHAT'S THAT WORD?

**Mesoamerica** is a historical and cultural region that extends from Mexico through Belize, Guatemala, El Salvador, Honduras, Nicaragua, and Costa Rica. For more than one thousand years, pre-Columbian societies grew and prospered in this part of the world, until the Europeans arrived.

Some settlers called smallpox a gift from God, who they believed wanted them to inhabit and tame the New World. In the early seventeenth century, one colonizing Puritan wrote: "The good hand of God . . . favored our beginnings in sweeping away great multitudes of the Natives by the smallpox."

Of course, the Europeans also died from the disease, sometimes in huge numbers. But in North America, they had the advantage over the Indigenous populations of more natural immunities to smallpox after centuries of outbreaks. And in some cases, European traders intentionally gave tribes blankets that had been infected with smallpox in order to increase the spread of the disease.

But the Native population of North America did not suffer solely by disease; they were drawn into numerous wars and were the victims of mass murder perpetrated by the European settler colonists.

There were multiple conflicts in places like Jamestown and other early colonies. The Pequot War of 1636–1638 in New England, between the Pequot tribe and a coalition of settlers and members of the Narragansett and Mohegan tribes, was the first sustained conflict between the settlers and the

Native Americans. For the first six months, the Pequot won every battle. But in an attack on a Pequot village, coalition forces burned the village, killing four hundred people. That was the turning point in a war that would see more English victories and the Pequot fleeing their homeland.

Another early war between the English settlers and the Native Americans is known as King Philip's War. King Philip is not who you might imagine: It is the Anglicized name given to Wampanoag chief Metacomet, who lived from 1638 to 1676. Metacomet, or Metacom, was the son of Wampanoag chief Massasoit, who had negotiated a peace treaty with the colonists. Metacom became chief of the Wampanoag Confederacy after his father and older brother died. The agreement his father had negotiated did not keep the colonists from stealing Indigenous lands. So there was already some serious tension between the Wampanoags and the colonists when three Wampanoags were hanged for the murder of another, following a trial held by the settlers, in 1675. That imposition of English law and justice on the Native community ratcheted up the tension tremendously, and war ensued, mostly in what is now Rhode Island and Massachusetts. It was brutal and very costly to both sides, with hundreds of colonists and thousands of Native Americans killed—including a massacre of the Narragansett tribe—and more Native Americans captured and enslaved. Dozens of colonist villages were burned and destroyed. But for the Native American population, the war really decimated the Wampanoag, Narragansett, and some smaller tribes in New England, enabling additional English settlements to rise up.

## WHAT'S THAT WORD?

*Anglicize* means to take a foreign word or name and make it sound English.

Metacomet was killed in the war, captured by a man named Benjamin Church and a Native American named John Alderman. American author Tommy Orange is a citizen of the Cheyenne and Arapaho Tribes of Oklahoma. In the prologue of his Pulitzer Prize–nominated novel, *There There*, he writes of what happened to Metacomet next.

> Metacomet was beheaded and dismembered. Quartered. They tied his four body sections to nearby trees for the birds to pluck. Alderman was given Metacomet's hand, which he kept in a jar of rum and for years took around with him—charged people to see it. Metacomet's head was sold to Plymouth Colony

for thirty shillings—the going rate for an Indian head at the time. The head was put on a spike, carried through the streets of Plymouth, then displayed at Plymouth Fort for the next twenty-five years.

There would be many conflicts and wars in the years following King Philip's War, and they all had something in common: the Europeans' determination to build more settlements and drive Indigenous people away or annihilate them. In the following pages, we will document some of the more significant wars and genocidal campaigns.

# CHAPTER 8
## AN AMERICAN GENOCIDE

*The great lie is that it is civilization. It's not civilized. It has been literally the most bloodthirsty, brutalizing system ever imposed upon this planet. That is not civilization. That's the great lie—is that it represents civilization.*

**—John Trudell (Santee Sioux poet and activist)**

In 2019, California governor Gavin Newsom issued a proclamation formally apologizing to Native Americans "for the many instances of violence, maltreatment, and neglect California inflicted on tribes." He also established the California Truth and Healing Council to help begin the healing process for Native Americans in the state.

During in-person remarks, the governor said something

seldom heard from American political leaders. "It's called a genocide. That's what it was. A genocide. [There's] no other way to describe it and that's the way it needs to be described in the history books," he said.

## WHAT'S THAT WORD?

**Genocide** is the murder of a large group of people from a particular nation, ethnic group, or religion with the goal of eliminating that group from existence or a particular location. You probably know the word from its association with the Holocaust during World War II, in which six million Jewish people were murdered. Columbia University professor Michael Witgen, a citizen of the Red Cliff Band of Lake Superior Ojibwe, says the genocide of Native Americans differs from the Holocaust in that there were multiple genocidal events and periods in history rather than one specific overarching policy like the Nazi's Final Solution. The Pequot War and King Philip's War are examples of genocidal events. But there are parallels as well, and Adolf Hitler, a name most frequently associated with the term genocide, referenced the treatment of Native Americans often when spelling out his plans to exterminate the Jewish people during World War II.

It is particularly poignant that the state of California issued a formal apology to Native people because of its brutal history. From the 1840s through the 1870s, some sixteen thousand Native Californians were killed in what can only be called a policy of genocide. California became a state in 1850 and immediately enacted a law that discriminated against Native people in multiple ways, including granting settlers the right to take Native children from their families.

But the settlers did much more than that, with the help of the state's government. The first governor of California was Peter Hardeman Burnett. In 1851, in a State of the State address, he said, "That a war of extermination will continue to be waged between the races until the Indian race becomes extinct must be expected."

A war of extermination was waged against Native Californians for the next couple of decades. State militias, army units, and ordinary citizens murdered and enslaved Native Americans, stole their property, and sent them into hiding on reservations, where many more died. It was all sanctioned and supported by the state. Up to 50 people killed at Goose Lake, nearly 260 murdered at Grouse Creek, and as many as 400 Pomo people murdered by the US cavalry and volunteer citizens near what is now San Francisco. The list goes on and on.

The Native population in California dropped from 150,000 people to about 30,000 in the middle of the nineteenth century. But this story is also one of survival against all odds: Today, California has the largest Native population in the country, with over 730,000 people, many of whom belong to 110 state tribes federally recognized by the US government.

While Governor Newsom used the word genocide, the United States has had an issue with admitting responsibility for the genocide it committed against its Indigenous people. Some other western nations that committed genocide against their Indigenous populations have since admitted guilt and promised reconciliation, including Canada and Australia. But the US government, despite mountains of evidence, to this day has refused to use the word genocide.

Why is that important? There are a couple of reasons.

If the United States uses the word genocide to describe its crimes against Native Americans, it will serve as an example to the rest of the world. In accepting responsibility, the United States might help prevent future persecution of

Indigenous people in other parts of the world. For example, in Brazil, many Indigenous people still live on their traditional homelands and speak traditional languages. But the rise of fascism under President Jair Bolsonaro, his history of racism against Indigenous people, and the government's pursuit of resources from their lands have put the lives and homelands of many Indigenous people at risk. Whether the United States can say anything that will impact Bolsonaro's actions is questionable. But US history has influenced him. In 1998, Bolsonaro told a newspaper, "It's a shame that the Brazilian cavalry hasn't been as efficient as the Americans, who exterminated the Indians." Jeffrey Ostler, who teaches history at the University of Oregon, says it has been particularly difficult for Americans to grapple with settler colonialism and the idea that the removal of Native Americans is fundamental to American history.

> It really is unsettling that if central to the foundation of the country was the idea of the fundamental entitlement to Native lands and then if in the process of acquiring those lands, there's not always, but consistently genocidal violence, at least the thread of it as I think there was, that's pretty unsettling to a narrative that says America is essentially good. And stands as a model of goodness to other countries.

Racism against Indigenous Americans is also widespread in the United States. An admission by the federal government of its history of atrocities against Native Americans will in theory allow us to voice the long list of grievances still affecting Indigenous people today, including the return of stolen lands and tribal sovereignty.

Apologies are a start, but they're not enough. Countries like Canada and Australia that have promised truth and reconciliation to Indigenous people have done little to follow through on such statements. Since Europeans first arrived in lands populated by Indigenous people, that betrayal of trust has been one of the most consistent markers of the relationship between settler colonists and Indigenous people. And if that cycle is to be broken, the United States and other countries in the Americas, and around the world, must admit to their atrocities and take action to address the grievances of Indigenous people.

## LET'S TALK ABOUT IT

* Can you think of any examples of racism that continue today toward Native Americans in the United States?

# CHAPTER 9
## NATIVE LAND, THE CHEROKEE NATION, AND THE TRAIL OF TEARS

At a theater in Pleasantville, New York, a narrator reads a few sentences that appear on screen before the start of each film, acknowledging that the theater sits on Munsee Lenape and Wappinger land. At the start of the Boston Marathon in 2021, the chairman of the Boston Athletic Association reads a statement acknowledging that the 26.2-mile race will run through the homelands of Indigenous people. On its website, Northwestern University acknowledges that it sits on the original lands of the Council of the Three Fires (Ojibwe, Potawatomi, Odawa).

A land acknowledgment is a formal statement by a

company or organization that recognizes and respects that Indigenous people are the original stewards of that land. It is a movement that has become more visible in recent years as more universities and corporations incorporate them into their communications. These statements are meant to express solidarity with Indigenous people, and acknowledge the injustices perpetrated against them throughout American history. Some Native Americans welcome the acknowledgments because land is so important to the history of Indigenous people in the Americas, and these statements can help undo the erasure of Indigenous people from a particular place.

## WHAT'S THAT WORD?

*Solidarity* means unity in an objective or a struggle. To be in solidarity means to stand with a group in word, action, or both.

"When we talk about land, land is part of who we are. It's a mixture of our blood, our past, our current, and our future. We carry our ancestors in us, and they're around us. As you all do," says Mary Lyons (Leech Lake Band of Ojibwe).

Others say such statements are performative and meaningless unless the company, organization, or individual takes additional actions.

## WHAT'S THAT WORD?

**Performative** is what it sounds like. It is often used in the realms of activism and social justice to imply that some people do things like share memes on Facebook or put up signs on their lawns to appear as though they are doing social justice work, when really it is more of a performance to make themselves look good. Of course, this can be subjective, and what is performative to one person might be true activism to another. Here are some things you can do to support Indigenous people that go beyond the performative:

- Donate money to Indigenous charities and organizations.

- Educate yourself about the land you are on, whether it's your school or your town.

- Support Indigenous artists and businesspeople by buying their products.

Whether or not you think land acknowledgments are helpful, it is important to acknowledge that in addition to focusing on the massacres of Native people, we also have to remember the forced removal of Native people from their lands. Native people believe that the land is available for the good of all people who share it. Some of our lands are considered sacred, including the burial places of our ancestors, which have some of the highest significance. And there's the way we have always viewed our interaction with the land. Regina Lopez-Whiteskunk, a member of the Ute Mountain Ute Tribe and advocate for land and water resources, explained it to True History.

> How I've been raised is, we're here to serve. We don't own the land; the land owns us. We serve and care for and provide stewardship for the land and all that comes from the land. We have great respect for the land, and we do what we can to protect and preserve that because it's all connected. We're all part of one ecosystem: our identity, our language, our way of life and connections to how we survive and how we conduct our ceremonies, everything is tied closely to the land. We don't own that.

Lopez-Whiteskunk says the idea of land ownership came with colonization. The Europeans looked at land in North America very differently, as a commodity: something to buy and sell, to cultivate agricultural products for sale, and as a means to wealth. They believed that it was their right to steal it, which they did starting with the earliest settlers, and throughout the following centuries. And once the United States was established, the federal government began to seize large-scale territories, starting with the Northwest Ordinance of 1787 and including legislation such as the Morrill Land-Grant College Act of 1862.

## HISTORY RECAP

**The Northwest Ordinance of 1787** created the Northwest Territory of the United States—the region west of Pennsylvania, north of the Ohio River, east of the Mississippi River, and south of the Great Lakes. It also established the precedent that allowed the government to expand westward and admit new states to the republic, rather than just expanding the existing ones. It negated any native titles to the land. In a conflict known as the Northwest Indian War, the Shawnee and Miami formed an alliance to stop white appropriation of their lands. In two battles, they killed eight hundred American soldiers. But as a result, President Washington authorized troops to launch an offensive against the Native people, and eventually this effort was successful.

**The Morrill Land-Grant College Act of 1862** enabled the US government to expropriate (seize from the owner) nearly eleven million acres of Indigenous lands from 245 tribal nations to build colleges and universities. Over time, the act was extended to every state and territory and resulted in schools like Cornell University, Purdue, and Florida State. That is just one example of the many times the US government seized Indigenous lands or broke treaty promises with Native Americans.

As the United States was forming, men in power understood the need to establish a relationship with Native people who had been living in North America long before they arrived. And in fact, the very first committee formed by Congress after the Revolution was the Administration of Indian Affairs, which Washington said "shall be directed entirely by the great principles of Justice and humanity." As president, he hoped the government could prepare some Native people to become full citizens. For example, Congress approved funding for agricultural education for men and women, and education for Native women in "domestic arts." The Cherokee were one of the "Five Civilized Tribes" selected, as they were believed to be the "model Indians," most likely to respond well to European belief systems.

But ultimately, Washington believed Indigenous people would have to assimilate or face extinction—they had no other options in his opinion. That justice and humanity Washington spoke of were not always at the forefront of his mind; acquiring land was the priority for Washington as both the president and a land speculator. And sometimes that priority resulted in violent conflicts with Indigenous people.

## WHAT'S THAT WORD?

*Assimilation* is the process by which a group or culture adopts the values, beliefs, languages, and behaviors of the culture in power. Sometimes this process occurs voluntarily—other times it's by force. Assimilation isn't inherently bad, but when it is subjected upon a minority group, it can be traumatic when the people in that group are forced to suppress their culture, and in many cases, abandon their native language.

According to Professor Witgen, "It isn't so much that Washington is set on incorporating Native people, assimilating them into the republic as citizens, as he's thinking about how to peacefully separate them from their land and incorporate that land into the republic."

## WHAT'S THAT PHRASE?

A *land speculator* in early America was someone who bought large swaths of land in anticipation that more settlers would come, enabling the speculator to sell off parcels for a profit.

Thomas Jefferson's point of view was motivated by the same desire for land. His goal was to push Native people to become farmers rather than hunter-gatherers. He believed once this was accomplished, they would realize they had more land than they needed and would see the value in selling it. He said if they couldn't get onboard with that project, they would have to be pushed out.

> There's definitely a strand of thought among the Revolutionary generation, where people like Thomas Jefferson believe that Native people can be assimilated. But the second generation of American public figures, led by Andrew Jackson, become the lead architects of a different idea: the idea of removal. They argue, "Look, we're a generation out after the Revolution, and Native peoples are not assimilating, not incorporating themselves into society." And they begin to articulate that this is why we have to have removal.

## II. A Policy of Removal

In the mid-nineteenth century, the tribes known as the Five Civilized Tribes—the Cherokee, Chickasaw, Choctaw, Muscogee, and Seminole—were recognized by the federal government as sovereign nations, free to govern themselves in accordance with their tribal laws. These tribes were in what today is known as the American Deep South. As settlers sprawled westward across the United States, they encroached on these tribal lands. Because the land was occupied, the settlers pressured the federal government to remove Natives from the land so they could claim it as their own. In response to the settlers' calls, President Andrew Jackson, who had long supported the removal of Native Americans, passed the Indian Removal Act (IRA) in 1830, which dissolved land ownership from the tribes.

Through this act, Jackson was able to grant lands east of the Mississippi to settlers in exchange for Native lands. In doing so, he forced Natives onto land west of the Mississippi. (To see a poster advertisement for these land grants, go to the photo insert.)

## HISTORY RECAP

**Andrew Jackson** was a lawyer in Nashville, Tennessee, who would later become a military general and ultimately the seventh president of the United States. His is the name most closely associated with the federal seizure of Indigenous lands.

Jackson's opinion of the Cherokee was common among white Tennesseans. He believed them to be a sore in the eye of colonization and that they would never become "civilized." As a military commander, he behaved brutally toward the dead after skirmishes with Native Americans. He once asked his men, "How many noses?" after ordering men to cut off the nose of every fallen warrior. Mutilation of dead bodies by white soldiers occurred frequently, across many parts of the United States. Interesting, isn't it, that this was a man who called others uncivilized.

This common way of thinking, that the Cherokee would never be civilized, was absurd, particularly when considering the white American standard of "civilized." The Cherokee nation was a thriving one that covered much of what is now Tennessee, Kentucky, Alabama, Virginia, Georgia, and the

Carolinas. Their capital was New Echota, near what is now Calhoun, Georgia, and in the early nineteenth century, they ratified a constitution modeled after the US Constitution, created a written language (invented by Sequoyah), and started a free press with a newspaper called the *Cherokee Phoenix*.

In a report for NPR's *This American Life*, journalist and author Sarah Vowell, who is of Cherokee descent, says they were a "nerdy, overachiever, bookish sort of tribe." Vowell continues, "More than any other Native American tribe, the Cherokees adopted the religious, cultural, and political ideals of the United States, partly as a means of self-preservation."

In the 1820s and '30s, Georgia passed a number of laws designed to undermine the Cherokee nation. They restricted Native Americans' rights to extract any wealth from their land, such as gold. The laws even banned all Native political assemblies, except when Cherokee were signing over land. The Cherokee fought back, using their newspaper to make their cause known and sending speakers across the country to plead their case. They lobbied Congress and created a petition that was signed by fifteen thousand tribe members. One of the Georgia laws eventually made its way to the Supreme

Court in the 1832 case *Worcester v. Georgia*, which declared the Cherokee a sovereign nation within the United States, and as a result, only answerable to federal law, not the state of Georgia. The Cherokee thought they had reason to celebrate.

But Andrew Jackson ignored that ruling and sent teams to survey Georgia lands for a land lottery. More and more white settlers arrived. Some tribes, like the Choctaw, Chickasaw, Seminole, and the Muscogee signed treaties requiring them to move to the other side of the Mississippi River, and they left. Divided on whether to stay or leave, the Cherokee stayed put and the majority decided to fight for their right to the land. President Jackson took advantage of the division that existed between those who wished to continue the fight and those who wanted to move on. And his government signed a treaty with one hundred Cherokee out of a sixteen-thousand-member tribe, even though they were by far the minority and had no authority to do so. The treaty gave them three years to get out.

It is important to note that the Bureau of Indian Affairs (formerly the Administration of Indian Affairs) at that time was part of the War Department, demonstrating that the government had always viewed Native people as an enemy.

President Jackson quickly replaced many top-ranking officials in the Bureau who didn't align with his policy on Native Americans. On May 28, 1830, Jackson signed the Indian Removal Act, which was used to forcibly remove thousands of people in what would later be known as the Trail of Tears.

### III. The Trail of Tears

The Trail of Tears of 1830 to 1840 was a death march in every sense of the phrase. More than seven thousand troops helped remove the Cherokee from their farms and homes. American troops first placed the refugees in stockades and forts. And then they were forced to move on.

The Cherokee were forced not only to leave their homes, but to make their way from Georgia and nearby regions to what is now Oklahoma, many on foot, eight hundred to one thousand miles. They started in the brutal summer heat and ended in the brutal cold of winter. It took four to six months. Sometimes they suffered from dehydration during drought. They suffered from starvation and fatigue. Not surprisingly, diseases spread among the displaced, so much so that the white soldiers enforcing the removal often camped far away, keeping their distance from the Native Americans. A new disease appeared on the trail called pellagra, and many more died from tuberculosis and pneumonia. There was no shelter provided along the way and parents and their children blistered in the sun by day and their teeth chattered in the cold of night.

Fifteen thousand people died on the Trail of Tears, buried along the way in unmarked graves. Throughout the trail in parts of Tennessee, Missouri, and other states, there are plaques honoring the dead. Many personal accounts speak of the overwhelming degree of death, combined with the heartache of being forced off ancestral homelands. People documented the daily tears wept in agony on the trail, which is where the name *Trail of Tears* comes from.

## LET'S TALK ABOUT IT

*So much of the persecution toward Native Americans is related to the land. Do you think the US government should consider returning stolen land to Native Americans?

# CHAPTER 10
## THE DAKOTA UPRISING AND THE GHOST DANCE AT WOUNDED KNEE

Before we examine the Dakota Uprising, also known as the Dakota War of 1862, we must take a step back and look at the bigger picture. Oftentimes, intense conflicts such as this one are the result of a series of harmful events committed over time. Eventually, things come to a head, usually resulting in violence. In the case of the Dakota Uprising, the foundation for war was laid long before the first drop of blood was ever shed.

First, you must understand the cultural differences between the Dakota people and the original European traders who settled in their region. For the Dakota people, as for many tribes of North America, generosity was a major cultural tradition. This meant that refusing someone in need was one of the greatest cultural taboos; it was essentially considered a sin. To the Dakota, generosity was valued even more than profit made from trade, and early on, they gave their resources to white settlers in need. Unfortunately, this value system conflicted with the market that white traders were looking to establish in Minnesota, and eventually left the Dakota with immense debts to traders and without goods to use themselves.

The Dakota people believed the debts they owed white settlers should dissolve in time due to that, especially given the way they gave in the name of generosity, expecting little in return, even when they were left without resources of their own (and did not have the privilege to write and receive more like white settlers could). As you'll see, this is an example of how capitalism is at the core of most major human rights violations in US history—the Dakota people had never before encountered a system where all resources were privately owned.

## WHAT'S THAT WORD?

**Capitalism** is an economic system where most means of trade and production are privately owned, as opposed to run by the state. Capital is another word for wealth. The United States functions as a capitalist country.

Instead of disappearing, these debts would become an integral part of the extensive operation that led to land belonging to the Dakota people being fraudulently obtained by the government to establish the state of Minnesota. In fact, Henry Hastings Sibley, Minnesota's first state governor, directly facilitated much of this fraud and embezzlement of funds.

In the mid- to late-seventeenth century, white settlers began arriving in Minnesota, which would later intensify pressure to "free up" Native lands for further white settlement. While working on major land deals and treaties to accommodate the near five thousand settlers who had come to the area by 1849, Governor Sibley and his agents skimmed funds that were meant to clear the Dakota people's debts with traders. When the land acquisition was set to be ratified by Congress, Sibley's partner Hercules Dousman confessed that 15 percent of the removal funds were used to bribe senators in Washington to ensure ratification. In geologist and historian Newton H. Winchell's 1911 study, he describes the Dakota treaties of 1851 as nothing more than a "monstrous conspiracy."

The Dakota treaties became some of the largest cash payouts for land ever made to Native Americans. But of the $250,000 a year promised to the people, much of it seemed to disappear into the pockets of white politicians and Indian Affairs agents. This ultimately left the Dakota people with no rights to hunt or fish on their traditional homelands and little land to live and grow food on. Eventually, resources from the government halted and the Indigenous population struggled to survive as they were in debt, out of money, and out of food.

By 1852, there was a continued influx of, now mainly German, settlers to Minnesota. With their arrival came a new attempt to seize land from the Dakota. The Dakota had already handed over most of their land in treaties that weren't upheld, and were now concentrated to a small reservation. Despite the Dakota people being unfairly herded to a tiny sector of space, the German settlers established the major town of New Ulm on reservation land anyway and encroached upon the Dakota even more. It quickly became clear to most Dakota that the promises of food and space in the treaties were never going to be held, as widespread corruption continued throughout the 1850s and their earlier generosity was made a mockery of.

According to accounts, the uprising began in August of 1862 when four Dakota warriors attempted to steal eggs from a white settlement and ended up killing members of a white family. When alerted about the incident, Dakota leaders came to the conclusion that war was inevitable and prepared their community. Years earlier, in June 1855, as their people continued to go hungry, Chief Little Crow and Chief Shakopee instructed their warriors to break into a warehouse and steal flour set aside for government workers without harming anyone. Before doing so, Dakota chiefs discussed whether it was possible for them to peacefully abandon their reliance on the corrupt government officials and return to hunting and fishing on their traditional homelands as a means of survival for their people. While many think only about the violence of the Dakota uprising, it is important to note that original intentions were of nonviolence, but the extreme circumstances led to an extreme response and the Dakota attack on New Ulm, trading posts, and agencies in the area. Still, media often went out of its way to show exaggerations of the uprising through examples of "Yellow Journalism" (an early form of "fake news," using sensational headlines to attract readers' attention).

Many of the first articles about the initial attacks on white settlers describe extremely exaggerated beheadings and other atrocious events that historians found no evidence or record of. Still, these false reports spread and horrified readers. By the uprising's end in late 1862, over 500 mostly newly arrived German and Scandinavian immigrants were dead, alongside nearly 150 Dakota warriors. This created a great panic and an exodus of white settlers from Minnesota. The abandonment of towns coupled with dramatic reporting from journalists put pressure on the government to act.

Governor Sibley sent the order to round up as many Dakota men as possible, convicting those gathered of crimes ranging from murder to rape, a completely unfounded accusation. Sibley initially proclaimed that any Dakota captured should be executed immediately, but would later learn that only the president of the United States could give such an order. Still, his hasty decision showed that from the beginning, any kind of legal due process (a right to a fair trial) was ignored, and many Dakota men accidentally incriminated themselves because of that. At Sibley's "trials," there was often no judge advocate present, and many of the accused would last only a matter of minutes.

Sibley then ordered some of his scouts to ride north and promise Dakota traveling west that only those who had committed crimes would be punished. This was a lie used to trick innocent people into trusting the scouts who led them into prison camps. The number of men charged reached 392. And in the end, 303 were condemned to death by Sibley's commission. Of those, 265 were convicted of being at a battle and 38 were convicted of killing civilians.

When Sibley's list was sent to President Lincoln for approval, Lincoln acknowledged to Congress the absence of a judge and suggested the possibility that a travesty of justice had occurred in the trials. He took a considerable amount of time requesting additional information on each case from Sibley and learned that near three hundred were tried in the same amount of time it would normally take to try one person. Though he took this into consideration and commuted most of the sentences, President Lincoln still signed off on the execution of all of the Dakota men convicted of killing civilians, despite the lack of evidence. Lincoln, who was coming up for reelection soon, was in no position to lose the state of Minnesota in the election, which most likely persuaded his decision.

In December of 1862, these thirty-eight Dakota men were hanged simultaneously in Mankato, Minnesota. As the Dakota men approached the gallows, they began to sing. Many Christian missionaries who had watched the whole situation play out cited the flagrant land theft and corruption by white politicians to be the true cause of the Dakota Uprising of 1862, but in the end, no white people were held responsible for the starvation of the Dakota people, the burning of Native American villages, or the embezzlement of funds.

In February 1863, Congress essentially canceled all treaties with the Dakota, ripping away all payments, food supplies, and any right to the land; many saw this as punishment to the remaining Dakota for the uprising. This remains the largest one-day mass execution in American history.

A few decades later, Native Americans would again be

massacred for resistance.

## II. The Ghost Dance at Wounded Knee

As white settlers continued to encroach westward upon their land, the outlook for many Native American communities was bleak. This led to the rise of many different spiritual visionaries throughout communities, most responding to the realization that the white man was bringing nothing but destruction for all Native American people. In the late 1800s, there emerged what became known as the Ghost Dance. Its exact origin is debated, but it is most widely attributed to the Northern Paiute visionary Wovoka, often referred to as "the Messiah." After a solar eclipse in 1889, Wovoka said, "When the sun died, I went up to heaven and saw God and all the people that had died a long time ago. God told me to come back and tell my people they must be good and love one another, and not fight, or steal, or lie. He gave me this dance to give to the people."

It was believed that if Natives rejected the customs adopted from white settlers and performed the Ghost Dance, God would return the animals to the land, remove white settlers from their territory, and return to earth loved ones who had died from disease and massacre. These ideas terrified white government officials and, even though there had never been any acts of violence attached to the Ghost Dance, it was deemed a threat. The government sent orders banning the Ghost Dance, but tribes practiced peaceful resistance by continuing to do it. It became prevalent on the Oglala Lakota Pine Ridge Reservation in South Dakota in response to widespread starvation and theft of land, but in communications between commissioners and agents on Pine Ridge, the dance was described as the "Messiah Craze" and the heightened and fearful communications signaled what was to come.

On December 29, 1890, tensions reached a boiling point when US soldiers surrounded a large group of Ghost Dancers at Wounded Knee and requested they stop dancing and hand over their weapons. When a scuffle between a Native American warrior and a white soldier ensued over a gun, a shot rang out and white soldiers opened fire, killing roughly 250 men, women, and children. For this act of genocide, the US military awarded the Medal of Honor, its highest commendation, to twenty of the soldiers who participated.

Today, the Ghost Dance and the massacre at Wounded

Knee are remembered as bloody examples of how the government massacred Indigenous people for practicing our culture and spirituality. But these are only two examples of what would become part of a much larger trend to destroy and eradicate the cultural identity of Indigenous people. Some white reformers would declare this cultural genocide to be "the Last Great Indian War."

In the years that followed these tragedies, the US government would adopt a new mantra, "kill the Indian in him, and save the man," to further their effort of complete ethnocide and genocide of Native Americans. It would begin with their children.

## LET'S TALK ABOUT IT

* Usually, we associate Abraham Lincoln with freedom and the end of slavery. But does your perception of him change when you realize that only one year before he signed the Emancipation Proclamation, he authorized a mass execution of Native American men?

# CHAPTER 11
## NATIVE AMERICAN BOARDING SCHOOLS

*It is admitted by most people that the adult savage is not susceptible to the influence of civilization, and we must therefore turn to his children . . . that they might be taught to abandon the pathway of barbarism and walk with a sure step along the pleasant highway of Christian civilization . . . They must be withdrawn, in tender years, entirely from the camp, and taught to eat, to sleep, to dress, to play, to work, to think, after the manner of the white man.*
—John H. Oberly, Indian School Superintendent, 1885

In May of 2021, an Indigenous community in British Columbia, a Canadian province, discovered roughly two hundred unmarked graves on the grounds of a former boarding school for Indigenous students. The graves are believed to hold the remains of missing children from the

Kamloops Indian Residential School, which operated from 1890 through the late 1970s. During this time more than 150,000 Indigenous children in Canada were forced to attend similar schools, most of them run by the Catholic Church. This discovery sparked other communities to search for similar gravesites using radar that can penetrate the ground without having to dig up the earth.

A month later, while Indigenous communities were still processing the sobering news of the Kamloops discovery, another burial site was found in the Canadian province of Saskatchewan. This time it was 600 graves. The site was on the former grounds of the Marieval Indian Residential School, which was in operation from 1898 until 1997.

The back-to-back discoveries are painful reminders of the brutality boarding schools imparted on Indigenous children and the legacy of the widespread institutional abuse that continues to affect Indigenous communities today.

But the roots of the boarding school system extend beyond Canadian borders to a system created by the United States government, whose mission was to strip Native Americans of their physical and cultural identities and force them to break ties to their families, tribes, and the land through the process of assimilation.

"I think when Americans hear the word 'school,' they think of something really positive," said Dr. Margaret Jacobs, a professor at the University of Nebraska–Lincoln, in an interview with the *New York Times*. Jacobs is a director at the Genoa Indian School Digital Reconciliation Project in Genoa, Nebraska, the former home of the Genoa Indian Industrial School, which operated from 1884 to 1934. "It's taken a while for Americans to realize that the boarding schools are not a benevolent institution, that they were set up to separate Indian children from their families and communities, to sever their ties," Jacobs said, and that it was time to confront "these really harsh histories." To fully understand the context and establishment of the harsh history of Native American boarding schools, we must first go further back in time.

As you read in Chapter 1, the root of the issue here, again, comes down to land ownership. Like Christopher Columbus who believed he was entitled to the land, as white European settlers made their way westward across the United States to claim land as their own, they ran into a similar problem: Native Americans were already living on the land. Rather than learn from the Natives who had been living on the lands for centuries prior to Columbus's arrival, the settlers, working with the federal government, forcibly pressured Natives to abandon land and, as a result, their culture. This is known as ethnocide, the deliberate destruction of a culture. Through a strategic government effort of various acts and laws throughout the nineteenth century, Native Americans were forcibly removed from their lands and onto reservations. Those who resisted relocation would be killed. But, as you'll learn, even those who succumbed to relocation didn't always survive. These forced relocations are part of the larger attempted genocide of Native Americans.

## WHAT'S THAT WORD?

A *reservation* is an area of land governed by a Native American tribal nation, not the government of the state in which it is located. By the time the US Constitution was ratified, the United States had recognized Native American tribal nations as being independent sovereign states, meaning they were free to govern themselves. But as more peace treaties were signed (many under duress and threat from the US government), Native American tribal nations were forced to surrender more land. Within these treaties, the government "reserved" certain parcels of land for Natives to live on. The term would remain in use as the government sought ways to forcibly remove Native Americans to designated lands that they had no historical connection with. Today, there are about 326 Native American reservations across the United States, the largest being the sixteen-million-acre Navajo Nation, which sprawls across Arizona, New Mexico, and Utah.

## II. The Makings of a Genocide

By the mid-1800s, white reformers began to despise the reservation system as it allowed Natives to maintain tribal life. And as they continued to settle on territories bordering Native reservations, conflicts arose with the neighboring tribal nations. The settlers did not believe they could coexist alongside the Natives. Many white Americans, including the government, believed that the only solution to the so-called "Indian problem" was the full assimilation of Native Americans into Euro-American culture.

As a solution to this "problem," Congress passed the Dawes Act (also known as the General Allotment Act) in 1887. The act effectively gave the American government legal authority to dissolve tribal ownership of reservations into individual allotments for Native American ownership. The policy was designed to further force assimilation by separating Natives from their tribes and making them American citizens.

These laws were praised by white reformers as they were part of a larger system that worked to dismantle tribal communities, free up land, and fund boarding schools. These schools would serve as yet another tool created by the federal government to eradicate Native American culture by forcing children to assimilate into the value systems of the Euro-American colonialists while abandoning their own cultural past and ways of life.

### III. The Native Home and Early Boarding School Experience

For Indigenous children in the United States, the assimilation process began as far back as the sixteenth century when schools run by Catholic missionaries were founded to teach Natives the ways of Anglo-European culture. But by the mid-nineteenth century, the federal government began funding these schools operated by the churches and created what came to be known as day boarding schools. At these schools, Native children would attend during the day but would return to their families in the evening.

In Native homes, children were considered gifts within the tribe. Elders cared for the children and nurtured their development, teaching them important life skills like hunting, gathering, and preparing food, and other cultural customs like putting out a tobacco offering before the taking of an animal. By acquiring these skills and customs, Native children learned to value themselves as important contributors to the tribe who were no more or less valuable than their elders. This would be in sharp contrast to the curriculum imposed at boarding schools, which was designed to "civilize" students and teach them the importance of private property and material wealth, among other values that conflicted with Indigenous culture.

The Northern Plains Reservation Aid (NPRA), a nonprofit organization dedicated to providing aid to impoverished Native communities, explains how the initial day boarding school system operated.

> The reservation day school had the advantage of being relatively inexpensive and caused the least opposition from parents. The reservation boarding school spent half a day

teaching English and academics and half a day on industrial training. Regimentation was the order of the day and students spent endless hours marching to and from classes, meals and dormitories. Order, discipline and self-restraint were all prized values of white society.

The boarding schools hoped to produce students that were economically self-sufficient by teaching work skills and instilling values and beliefs of possessive individualism, meaning you care about yourself and what you as a person own. This opposed the basic [Native] belief of communal ownership, which held that the land was for all people.

—From nativepartnership.org

But, in the eyes of the educators and the government, there was a flaw with these missionary-run schools: after school ended, Indigenous children returned to their reservations, to their families, where they spoke their Native language, wore their Native clothing, and practiced their tribal ways at home. As historian Ronald Naugle puts it, "The reservation environment, to which the child returned daily, undermined the process of assimilation."

The second attempt by the federal government to facilitate a more successful assimilation came in the form of reservation boarding schools, where children would only be allowed to visit their families on holidays and during the summer. Again, these proved that schools were ineffective, as Native children were still in contact and influenced by their families during these limited visits. By the late nineteenth century, the "Indian problem" had become a federal priority. The federal government looked to Captain Richard Henry Pratt, a former military leader, for solutions.

## IV. Off-Reservation Boarding Schools

In 1879, Pratt received federal funding to establish the Carlisle Indian Industrial School in Carlisle, Pennsylvania. Carlisle was an off-reservation boarding school where Native students would not be able to visit their families and would commit to a minimum of four years of school. Carlisle became the largest, most visible model of the off-reservation boarding school. For the next twenty-five years, Pratt was one of the most outspoken figures advocating for the expansion of Native American boarding schools. He believed that these off-reservation schools should be built in white communities so that Native Americans could observe the "advanced" level of the white communities. By 1908, there were twenty-seven off-reservation boarding schools that were fully funded and operated by the Bureau of Indian Affairs, and more than three hundred other schools that received support from the US government. By the late 1920s, nearly 83 percent of all

Native American students were enrolled in this model of schooling. Following Pratt's direction, the US government believed that if Native children were removed from their culture and placed in an Anglo one, they would successfully assimilate within one generation.

As more Natives were forced from their land and onto reservations, living conditions for Native people declined dramatically as they no longer were on familiar land that they could cultivate and thrive. Life on these reservations was horrible. Starvation, disease, and death became commonplace. And most Natives were living in poverty. Because of these poor conditions, Native families were willing to send their children to these types of boarding schools that promised them a better life. Even Tribal leaders sent their children to boarding schools to learn "white man ways" as they feared it was the only way of survival of their tribe.

Assimilation of Native children into the dominant Anglo-European culture relied on a methodical, militaristic approach—one that Pratt was familiar with. With the establishment of Carlisle, the US government had begun a complete cultural cleansing, or ethnocide, of Indigenous children by removing them from their family units and attempting to instill the Christian values of the Anglo-Europeans. Through Carlisle, the US government was committed to effectively carrying out Pratt's ambition to "Kill the Indian in him, and save the man."

## V. The Boarding School Experience

Upon arrival at boarding schools, many children were subjected to the "Gospel of Soap," the washing away of children's dirt and grime, often from the long journey to get to the school. What might seem like an innocent act was just the first way for the school leadership to attack the children's identity and culture, by suggesting that they were "dirty" and needed to be "cleaned." In a 1994 PBS documentary called *Nokomis: Voices of Anishinabe Grandmothers*, an Ojibwe woman named Esther Nahgahnub, who attended an off-reservation boarding school, shares her story:

> This teacher drove all the way out to where we lived and complained to my stepmother in outraged terms that my hands were dirty. And that was one of the few times that I'd ever seen [my stepmother] mad. And I still remember her words: "God made her that color and you and no amount of soap is going to change her." . . . But my dad felt so bad about it that he thought he would try to do something for me. So, he began to try to bleach me with lemon.

Esther's story highlights the unfortunate lengths parents were willing to go in their attempts to assimilate their children. (To watch the documentary in its entirety, go to the Selected Bibliography on page 176 for more information.)

Shortly after the children's arrival, school leaders would then cut off their hair. To Native people, growing long hair is a sacred tradition and a great source of pride and honor. Many Native children had never before cut their hair.

In 1921, Zitkála-Šá, a Dakota woman born on the Yankton Indian Reservation in South Dakota, wrote a collection of short essays called *American Indian Stories*, detailing her boarding school experience. In one essay, "The Cutting of My Long Hair," Zitkála-Šá records her traumatic experience upon arrival at the boarding school and having her hair cut.

I cried aloud, shaking my head all the while until I felt the cold blades of the scissors against my neck, and heard them gnaw off one of my thick braids. Then I lost my spirit. Since the day I was taken from my mother I had suffered extreme indignities. People had stared at me. I had been tossed about in the air like a wooden puppet. And now my long hair was shingled like a coward's! In my anguish I moaned for my mother, but no one came to comfort me. Not a soul reasoned quietly with me, as my own mother used to do; for now I was only one of many little animals driven by a herder.

This was another cruel act to erase the children's physical identity while also stripping them of their cultural past. Assimilation was more than just the physical destruction of culture.

Educators would then change the children's names to more "American" sounding ones, effectively ending a Native child's family's lineage. Children were instructed to forget their traditional names given by their families in exchange for white, Christian names. Teachers believed that a good "American" sounding name would better prepare them for mainstream society. Many names were chosen from the Bible while others were crude translations of the child's given name. This changing of names robbed children of their sense of self and severed ties with their longstanding ancestral lineage.

Even the physical structures of the boarding school facilities were designed to eradicate the memory of any Native American cultural ties. The buildings were typically long and linear as were the rooms. Tables within the facilities were also intentionally designed to have the same effect. This design was in great contrast to Native Americans' use of circular space, like with the Sacred Hoop, which represents the interconnectedness of everything in creation.

But perhaps the most culturally destructive act enforced at boarding schools was the policy forbidding children to speak their Native language; they were only allowed to speak English. This policy was strictly enforced, and, if broken, children were subject to various degrees of punishments, typically in the form of physical abuse.

Living conditions at these schools were unsanitary as children were forced into tight, overcrowded rooms where diseases like tuberculosis, influenza, and smallpox could easily spread. Many schools had their own cemeteries, and it was the students who were tasked with building their classmates' coffins. Because of this, many Native children attempted to run away. The practice became so common that some schools offered bounties (money) for the return of runaway children. Unsurprisingly, these schools would become institutions that encouraged the widespread humiliation, shaming, and physical abuse of Native children—a far cry from the way we view school today.

Despite the all-out war conducted on our cultural ways in these boarding schools, many forms of counterculture resistance by students took place. Some children would tie feathers to their bed at night to stay connected with their spirituality. Some spoke their traditional languages to each other in secret. There were even incidents of arson and sabotage by students running away from schools and making one final statement about school life. When some students graduated and returned to their reservations, they would continue to practice their former way of life in an attempt to reclaim their cultural identity.

## VI. The Legacy of Carlisle
## and the Resilience of Natives

In 1918, after thirty-nine years in operation, Carlisle Indian Industrial School closed its doors. Over twelve thousand Native children had entered as unique individuals and as members of a culture with distinct customs and traditions that had been passed down from one generation to the next. Upon entering and leaving Carlisle, these young people, like thousands of others in similar boarding schools, were forced to abandon that culture and break their lineage by changing their name, cutting their hair, and forgetting their Native language. It wouldn't be until 1996 that the last government-funded off-reservation school, Gordon's Indian Residential School in Saskatchewan, Canada, would close. Through acts of rebellion and resistance, many were able to survive, but they still carry the physical and emotional scars of their time.

Take, for instance, the story of Joe Buffalo, a professional skateboarder from Alberta, Canada, and a member of the Samson Cree tribal nation, who attended residential school. In 2021, Joe Buffalo was the star of a documentary film called *Joe Buffalo*, produced by legendary skateboarder Tony Hawk. (To watch the film, visit the Selected Bibliography on page 176.) But before he went pro, Joe Buffalo, like so many other young Natives growing up in Canada, was forced to attend a boarding school.

> I wasn't able to communicate with my parents. I got to see them like once or twice a year. There were two hundred and fifty kids in a room with bunk beds. So, you could hear kids crying. You could hear a lot of things at night. I could hear spirits in the walls from the dark history there. Who are you supposed to run to when you say, "Mom, Dad," you know? Who's going to come and protect me from these people? . . . But the severity of what I've gone through is nothing compared to what my parents or my grandparents have gone through.

When Joe Buffalo was fifteen, he left the school for Ottawa, Canada, where he was soon accepted into a new culture: skateboarding. Today, Joe Buffalo uses his story and platform to educate Canada's youth: "I want to get the point across to the kids that if I can make it happen, given the circumstances of how I was raised, then there's hope out there."

And though it will never undo the brutality that thousands of Native children and families endured and continue to endure to this day, the US government has finally begun to publicly acknowledge the brutality of boarding schools, providing some measure of hope for future generations.

In 2009, Congress passed a joint resolution "to acknowledge a long history of official depredations and ill-conceived policies by the Federal Government regarding Indian tribes and offer an apology to all Native Peoples on behalf of the United States." The legislative passage continues:

> The ancestors of today's Native Peoples inhabited the land of the present-day United States since time immemorial and for thousands of years before the arrival of people of European descent. . . . The Federal Government condemned the traditions, beliefs, and customs of Native Peoples and endeavored to assimilate them by such policies as the redistribution of land under the Act of February 8, 1887 (commonly known as the "General Allotment Act"), and the forcible removal of Native children from their families to faraway boarding schools where their Native practices and languages were degraded and forbidden.

And in another rare admission of public apology, in 2016 the United States Army met with the Northern Arapaho Tribe and the Sicangu Lakota to discuss the repatriation of children buried at Carlisle. Repatriation means to return a person home to their own country or land. The US Army agreed to pay for the buried children's exhumations and transport back to their Native lands. This is the first boarding school repatriation to date.

Five years later, in 2021, Deb Haaland, the first Native American to serve as a cabinet secretary, announced the Federal Indian Boarding School Initiative to review the legacy of boarding schools. Haaland explained that "the Interior Department will address the inter-generational impact of Indian boarding schools to shed light on the unspoken traumas of the past, no matter how hard it will be. I know that this process will be long and difficult. I know that this process will be painful. It won't undo the heartbreak and loss we feel. But only by acknowledging the past can we work toward a future that we're all proud to embrace."

And in an op-ed for the *Washington Post* that same year, Haaland shared her family's experience with boarding schools: "My maternal grandparents were stolen from their families when they were only 8 years old and were forced to live away from their parents, culture and communities until they were 13. Many children like them never made it back home," Haaland wrote. Her great-grandfather was taken to

Carlisle Indian Industrial School.

Despite the recent discoveries of the multiple unmarked gravesites in Canada and the American government finally acknowledging the brutality of Native American boarding schools, these discoveries leave us with the pain and the memory of what our grandparents and great-grandparents for generations and generations had to survive. And there has yet to be a true reconciliation made by the US federal government to acknowledge this genocide.

To us it's deeper than just the lives of these children. These programs have a lasting effect on our communities, our family units, and the emotional trauma we still live with today. We have survived everything thrown our way, but that doesn't mean we don't carry the scars of genocide. Knowing that this brutal history is still impacting us and our families to this day. Yet most the world only perceives us as a people of the past—simply a historical symbol of America. We are a people *with* a past but we do not live solely in the past.

Today our cultural pride is a testament to that survival, a testament to the fact that they failed to fully break our spirit and our connection to the land and our people.

We are resilient.

## LET'S TALK ABOUT IT

* Can you think of times in your own life when you had to assimilate into a certain culture or social setting to better fit in? Explain.

# CHAPTER 12
## THE RISE OF THE AMERICAN
## INDIAN MOVEMENT (AIM)

In the summer of 1968 in Minneapolis, Minnesota, a local grassroots movement that would soon take hold nationally was born: the American Indian Movement. A grassroots movement is one where the people, like locals of a community, come together to make political and social change. Though these movements typically begin small, they can achieve great leaps of progress. And to fully understand the American Indian Movement, you have to look at the life of Dennis Banks, one of its founding members, and the racism that existed then and still exists today in Minnesota toward Native Americans.

After eleven years in Christian boarding schools, without any contact with his family, Dennis successfully escaped at the age of sixteen, with his friend Bojack. By seventeen, Dennis enlisted in the air force as a way to make sure he had both three meals a day and a place to sleep. Enlisting became one of the only ways for many young Native American men at the time to ensure their basic needs were met. While stationed in Japan, Dennis fell in love with a local girl named Machiko, and after two years of dating, she became pregnant with his child. Not long after the military ordered him to return to the United States to be discharged, Dennis, now a new father, requested to be discharged in Japan, but the military refused. Left with few options, Dennis took Machiko and his newborn child and went AWOL meaning absent without leave.

Their time on the run was short lived and Dennis was arrested soon thereafter. After risking his life and serving his country overseas, he returned to the United States in chains for the crime of being in love. Falling on hard times upon his return, Dennis lost track of Machiko and his young daughter. Eventually, he made his way back to Minnesota, ending up in the Native American ghettos of Minneapolis–St. Paul.

He recalled that every spring, the local police targeted only Native American men, rounding up around two hundred men a week to work as government-sanctioned slave laborers, cleaning convention centers and other seasonal venues for city projects. The police would only target bars frequented by Native Americans, pulling up behind the establishments with a wagon and then going to the front and pushing everyone out the back and into the vehicle. They arrested people without any cause or evidence of crimes committed. Men were herded like cattle, usually charged with being "drunk and disorderly," even if the accused was completely sober. Dennis recalls being caught in this dragnet twenty-five times. Eventually, Dennis himself ended up in state prison. While working a minimum wage job and unable to provide for his large family, he had turned to stealing food. His accomplice in the crime was a white man named Bill. Though they were both arrested for the crime, Dennis was sentenced to five years in state prison but Bill was only sentenced to two years' probation and was released immediately.

It was during his time at Minnesota Correctional Facility at Stillwater that Dennis began focusing on researching Native history and became politicized. He was taking note of the growing antiwar and civil rights movements in the United States and yearned to be a part of a movement for Native American rights. He quickly realized there were already nineteen Native American organizations in Minnesota, mainly dealing with social welfare and gathering clothes, but none addressed police harassment, social reform, human rights, or treaty rights. Upon his release from prison in May of 1968, Dennis contacted his old friend from boarding school, George Mitchell, about starting a movement. On July 28, 1968, the American Indian Movement was officially founded. The first meeting was organized in the basement of a run-down church. Many of the attendees of the first meeting voiced similar concerns about police harassment, specifically at the Native bars on Franklin Avenue, so they decided to establish a patrol to monitor police harassment in Native American neighborhoods, patterned after the Black Panthers in Oakland, California. They painted three old cars red and began the first AIM patrols to document police brutality. These patrols became a way to intervene in instances of extreme police violence. Warriors armed themselves and patrolled the streets protecting many Native organizations, businesses, and homes.

# DELIA DESCHAMP AND HER FAMILY, CIRCA MID-NINETEENTH CENTURY

Front left: Delia Deschamp, the author's great-great-great grandmother. After Delia's father died when she was two years old, Delia was put up for adoption and placed with a white family, where she was forced to abandon her Native culture. She would later reconnect with her mother, Susan Sawyer (back center), and embrace her true Native ways.

# MAP OF THE
# HAUDENOSAUNEE CONFEDERACY

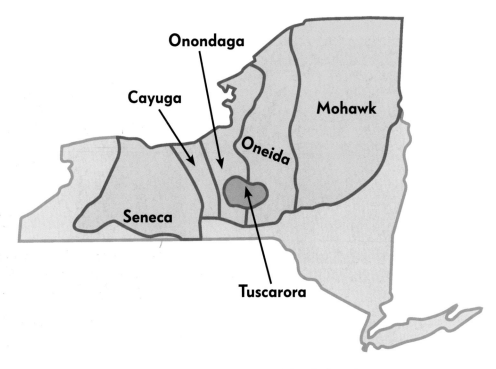

Onondaga

Cayuga

Mohawk

Oneida

Seneca

Tuscarora

The original five nations—Mohawk, Oneida,
Onondaga, Cayuga, and Seneca—were later
joined by the Tuscarora as the sixth nation in 1722.

# NATIVE AMERICANS AT CARLISLE INDIAN INDUSTRIAL SCHOOL, PENNSYLVANIA

An 1879 photo of Dakota boys arriving at
Carlisle Indian Industrial School in Pennsylvania

A 1915 photo of the Carlisle Indian Industrial School Band.
The school closed three years later.

Advertisements like this were made possible when President Andrew Jackson passed the Indian Removal Act of 1830, which effectively dissolved land ownership by Native American tribes and made it available to colonial settlers.

# PROPAGANDA IN ART

## THE LANDING AT PLYMOUTH ROCK, DECEMBER 1620

This print (circa 1845) shows a Native American welcoming colonial settlers, including some of the Pilgrims of Plymouth Colony. Here the white settlers are depicted as brave heroes crossing the uncharted waters while Native Americans welcome them to shore.

## THE LANDING OF COLUMBUS

An 1846 painting of Columbus raising the Spanish flag while Native Americans can be seen in the distant background. It would be hard not to see the artist's depiction of Columbus as anything less than a god, as he is surrounded by men kneeling and praying to him and a crucifix of Jesus.

# PROPAGANDA IN PRINT

Originally published in *Harper's Weekly* on December 28, 1878, this illustration, titled "Patience Until the Indian *Is* Civilized—So to Speak," explains the American government's policy toward Native Americans. The caption reads: "Secretary of the Interior. 'There are two methods of Indian management possible: either to herd and coral [sic] the Indians under the walls or guns of a military force, so to speak, so as to watch them and prevent outbreaks; or to start them at work upon their lands, to educate them, and to civilize them......There are in the Army a great many gentlemen who have good ideas about the Indian Service, but it is one thing to have ideas, and another to carry them out, and I think that the patient labor and care of detail necessary to raise the Indian tribes to a state of civilization would not be found among the officers of the Army.'"

# ZITKÁLA-ŠÁ

Zitkála-Šá (1876–1938) was a Dakota woman and author of *American Indian Stories*, where she documented her traumatic experiences at boarding school and having her sacred long hair cut. She became a prominent political activist for women's and Native American rights.

# THE EXECUTION OF THIRTY-EIGHT DAKOTA NATIVE AMERICANS

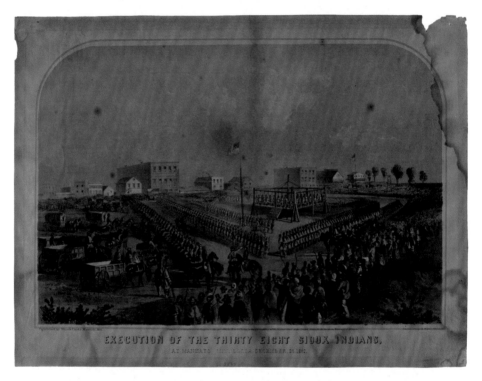

EXECUTION OF THE THIRTY EIGHT SIOUX INDIANS,

On December 26, 1862, thirty-eight Dakota people were executed in Mankato, Minnesota, surrounded by soldiers and spectators. This execution, the largest one-day mass execution in US history, would eventually lead to the Dakota Uprising.

It's important to recognize that around the time of AIM's formation in Minnesota, Native Americans made up only 10 percent of the population in Minneapolis but represented almost 70 percent of the jail population in the city. Logically, AIM brought up this statistic directly to the Minneapolis police chief at the time and he responded, saying, "Naw, there's no racism here." This was untrue as arrest records showed that not only did racism exist but the city of Minneapolis even used to have separate sentencing guidelines for Native Americans written into its laws. The separate set of guidelines required harsher punishments for the same crimes solely based on the citizens' race. This blatant example of systematic racism is why many Native people refer to Minnesota, Wisconsin, and the Dakotas as the "Deep North," a parallel to the more commonly known Jim Crow laws of the Deep South. (To learn more about these laws and systemic racism in America, read *The Legacy of Jim Crow*, another book in the True History series.)

In the beginning, Dennis was committed to ensuring AIM remained a nonviolent movement. AIM, from its creation, always kept its roots in traditional Native American culture and spirituality. Eventually, because of the constant contact with heavily armed police, the need for what they called "necessary violence" became more evident. As AIM outgrew Minneapolis, they became the national Native rights "fire brigade" in multiple ways. AIM would typically receive a call from a Native community experiencing violence or other injustices and would then put out a national call to action to all their chapters to converge on that specific tribal community. This began the "stand-up" approach to Native activism.

AIM, alongside other groups, occupied various high-profile locations, including a former federal prison on Alcatraz Island in California for nineteen months, from November 1969 to June 1971. In 1972, AIM members occupied the Bureau of Indian Affairs building in Washington, DC. Things came to a head in February of 1973 on the Oglala Lakota Pine Ridge Reservation in South Dakota, at the site of the Wounded Knee massacre. The Oglala Lakota people had become fed up with the tyranny and violent oppression from their then tribal president Dick Wilson. Wilson had blatantly rigged tribal elections and squashed any opposition to him with weaponry allegedly provided to him by the US government. He even openly referred to his paramilitary death squad as the "Goon Squad."

Wilson ruled by fear and violence, burning people's homes and shooting people in the dead of night. Neither FBI nor other federal agents were observed showing any motivation to intervene and stop the murders. Naturally, AIM was called to Pine Ridge by the traditional leaders of the community that was facing the brunt of the violence. After a meeting between AIM and community leaders, it was determined a stand would be taken at Wounded Knee, the site of one of America's greatest human rights violations, where around 250 Lakota people were killed by soldiers of the US Army on December 29, 1890. The site was being operated by a white family as a tourist attraction, where visitors could buy knock-off Native American memorabilia. AIM, along with local community members, began an armed occupation of the town. The town was quickly surrounded by armed federal agents and Dick Wilson's Goon Squad.

After holding "the knee" for seventy-one days, many of AIM's top leadership were either arrested or forced underground, utilizing a sophisticated network of activists. They also took refuge in sovereign Native American nations. Dennis was able to escape capture, and he and his family were eventually taken in by the Onondaga Nation. He ultimately felt confined by the reservation borders and turned himself in, over a decade after the stand at Wounded Knee. In one of the infamous AIM trials, it was disclosed that the US military was involved in the operations at Wounded Knee, a violation of the Posse Comitatus Act of 1878, which prevents the president from using the military as a domestic police force against its citizens.

Because of the national attention gained from these actions, many Americans who had rarely paid attention to Native issues were forced to acknowledge the oppression Native Americans continued to experience. As a result, some changes were made to federal laws in the late 1970s following the rise of AIM, like the American Indian Religious Freedom Act (AIRFA) and the Indian Child Welfare Act (ICWA). The ICWA was meant to address the mass removal of Native children from households by government welfare workers and private agencies. Unsurprisingly, this welfare and adoption system had become another tool for assimilation and colonization by the US government.

## THE AMERICAN INDIAN RELIGIOUS FREEDOM ACT

In 1978, Congress passed the American Indian Religious

Freedom Act (AIRFA), which provided protection for Native Americans to access ceremonial and religious sites, to use and possess sacred objects, and to worship through ceremonials and traditional rites. Take note, an entire act had to be passed to ensure Native Americans' rights they should have already been protected by the First Amendment of the US Constitution, which guarantees all citizens the freedom of speech, religion, press, assembly, and the right to petition the government. Previously, the US government's policy was largely based on the dominant Christian perspective that all Native religious practices were simply "superstitious," and therefore not valid religions protected under the First Amendment. AIRFA detailed access to sacred sites for ceremonial purposes, protocols concerning the discovery of Native artifacts and burial sites, and the sacramental use of peyote, which Native Americans have used for thousands of years.

Though it began as a small grassroots movement, the American Indian Movement would have a profound influence on all Native activism that followed, laying the foundation for a powerful spirit of resistance that is still alive and well today.

# CHAPTER 13
## LAND ACTIVISM AND ENVIRONMENTALISM

*The air is foul, the waters poisoned, the trees dying, the animals are disappearing. We think even the systems of weather are changing. Our ancient teaching warned us that if Man interfered with the Natural Laws, these things would come to be. When the last of the Natural Way of Life is gone, all hope for human survival will be gone with it. And our Way of Life is fast disappearing, a victim of the destructive processes . . . The people who are living on this planet need to break with the narrow concept of human liberation, and begin to see liberation as something which needs to be extended to the whole of the Natural World. What is needed is the liberation of all the things that support Life—the air, the waters, the trees— all the things which support the sacred web of Life.*

This quote is from a 1977 address delivered to the United Nations in Geneva, Switzerland, at a conference called

"Discrimination Against Indigenous Populations of the Americas." Representatives from the Haudenosaunee presented papers from John Mohawk, Chief Oren Lyons, and José Barreiro, in which they called for a "consciousness of the Sacred Web of Life in the Universe," a call that they "expected to be both ignored and misunderstood for some period of time."

The representatives were right: Their calls were ignored. And since their address, we have seen unprecedented destruction to the environment on a global scale. From intense droughts to rising sea levels, melting glaciers to larger wildfires, massive storms to rolling heat waves, climate change is here, and much of it is directly caused by humans in their never-ending quest for more land, resources, and money.

Nearly fifty years after that Geneva conference, as the world and the United States still grapple with environmental destruction to the earth's air, soil, and water, Indigenous communities are disproportionately impacted by climate change. Since Europeans began colonizing the United States, Indigenous people have lost 99 percent of their historical tribal land base. As a result, they have been forced to live in areas that are more exposed to extreme heat, drought, and other negative effects of climate change, according to a multiyear study published in the journal *Science*.

"The reason why tribal nations are located in the places they are is because the U.S. tried to remove them and get them out of the way, so that the U.S. could build this massive industrial economy, that we now know contributes to increased concentrations of increased greenhouse gasses in the atmosphere," says Kyle Whyte, one of the study's coauthors.

Ironically, Indigenous communities are the very ones who have long been living in peace with nature. And these are the communities that continue to fight for the protection of the earth and climate justice.

## WHAT'S THAT PHRASE?

*Climate justice* means the fair treatment of all people in the creation of policies that affect our natural resources and policies to combat climate change. Certain racial groups, including Indigenous Americans, Black Americans, and Latinx Americans are often victims of climate *injustice*. People who live in poverty often live near coal-fired plants and landfills, in parts of the country where water is unsafe or scarce, or where the air is more polluted by factories. Activists and politicians who work toward climate justice seek healthy water and air for all people, regardless of their background, race, or income level. But government policies often do just the opposite.

You may have heard of the Dakota Access Pipeline (DAPL). DAPL is a 1,172-mile-long underground oil pipeline that begins in northwest North Dakota and runs southeast until Patoka, Illinois. Pipelines, which transport oil, are known to burst and can cause widespread environmental damage, like poisoning bodies of drinking water.

The company Energy Transfer originally designed the pipeline to route through Bismarck, North Dakota, the state's capital, where over 90 percent of the inhabitants were white. The Bismarck route was rejected as it was deemed unsafe for Bismarck's water supply. The pipeline was then rerouted to avoid Bismarck, instead passing through the nearby Standing Rock Sioux Reservation, home to the Lakota and Dakota people (collectively known as the Sioux). The people of Standing Rock were against the construction of the pipeline because it would cross under the Missouri and Mississippi rivers as well as Lake Oahe, just east of the reservation. The Sioux considered the construction of the pipeline a serious threat to the drinking water of millions of people, as well as a threat to ancient Indigenous burial grounds and cultural sites.

In 2016, youth from Standing Rock and surrounding Native American communities organized a campaign called "ReZpect Our Water" to stop the pipeline. As the campaign grew, the Lakota phrase "Mni Wichoni," or "Water is Life" became the anthem from Standing Rock, and the people who participated called themselves water protectors, rather than protestors.

A water protectors' camp was set up, and the movement grew to include members of over one hundred Indigenous tribes and other supporters from around the world. The water protectors used social media to get out their message, and it worked. Their efforts became a national and international news story for months, and garnered support, sympathy, and financial contributions from millions of Americans who could see the social injustice of the Dakota Access Pipeline in real time on their phones and TVs. In September of 2016, for example, guard dogs and pepper spray were used to hold back the peaceful protestors, some of whom were bitten and bloodied. In other cases, protestors were arrested. Some politicians, including President Barack Obama and Senator Bernie Sanders, supported the movement as well.

The water protectors made some real progress during the Obama administration, under which the Army Corps of Engineers temporarily blocked the company from building the pipeline under the Missouri River. But it was too late. When President Donald Trump came into office a few months later, he reversed that decision. Despite the monthslong campaign and numerous legal attempts to overturn the project, Indigenous voices were ignored, and DAPL was completed in 2017.

This is an example of environmental racism, another of the many issues Native communities continue to face today. As you've learned in previous chapters, the American government has a long history of willfully ignoring Indigenous voices and perspectives.

## A CLOSER LOOK: ALASKA

For many Indigenous people, the land and water

provide their daily food. In Alaska, where 18 percent of the population is American Indian or Alaska Native according to the 2014 census, Native people often practice a traditional, subsistence lifestyle of hunting, fishing, and food gathering in remote areas with harsh climates. Fishing is particularly vital to so many Indigenous communities in the state. In fact, the word *Alaska* comes from an Unangam Tunuu word that means "place the sea moves toward." But as Alaska's climates have been changing, Indigenous communities' resources have diminished in some locations. A case in point is along the Yukon River in the Yukon Flats, where 94 percent of families rely on salmon fishing, not only for their food but for their cultural survival. Warming seas have negatively impacted the salmon runs in the Yukon, and governmental regulations have often favored commercial fisherman over the Indigenous communities there.

Climate change is also forcing more than thirty Native Alaskan communities to face the prospect of relocation as temperatures rise, arctic ice melts, and coasts erode. As of this writing, four tribes have already been forced to relocate, and the people affected say the US government is not doing enough to help them or others who face the same fate. In 2020, five tribes from Alaska and Louisiana, where flooding also poses a threat to Indigenous life, filed a complaint with the United Nations that says the United States is failing to address the impacts of climate change that are forcing them to move from homes their ancestors have lived in for thousands of years.

But sometimes Indigenous environmental activists are successful. The Bears Ears and Grand Staircase-Escalante national monuments in Utah are examples of a positive outcome. In 2017, Trump's Department of the Interior had reduced the protected area around Bears Ears by 85 percent, a devastating blow to the tribes who have stewarded that land for thousands of years. There are thousands of cultural artifacts at Bears Ears, such as ancient cliff dwellings and Indigenous rock art. These artifacts were left undisturbed until European settlers began to explore the area in the mid-nineteenth century, when Indigenous people were forcibly removed from the land.

Land advocates like Regina Lopez-Whiteskunk, a citizen of the Ute Mountain Ute tribe and former cochair of the Bears Ears Inter-Tribal Coalition, led the efforts to regain protections for these lands. And, in 2021, the Biden administration listened to Native Americans and reversed the

Trump decision, reinstating the boundaries of the protected area (1.35 million acres) established by President Obama and adding more acreage to it.

It was a clear victory for Lopez-Whiteskunk and many other people who had been fighting for this region for years. But there is always the concern that another president could reverse those protections again, and activists have been lobbying for permanent protections for these areas. Lopez-Whiteskunk says it's difficult to trust the government:

"When we think about our history and relationship to being Native American, we have always had that history of things being difficult, of things having to be a fight, and when it seems like movement in the right direction, it doesn't always mean that's how it's going to stay."

This is an effort to protect land—which is rich in cultural history and has many uses to the Native people of the Southwest—not to reclaim it. She says the coalition is not saying that they're entitled to own these lands. They want to see them fully protected by the federal government. It is where life has always occurred for her people, for her ancestors. And she says everything is tied to the land.

Lopez-Whiteskunk says when the government takes

away land from Indigenous people, it is an act of genocide. You might find that a surprising use of the word genocide. You'll remember we learned about its meaning in Chapter 8 when discussing how European settlers killed so many Native Americans in their efforts to control the land. But how is taking land from people genocide? We asked Lopez-Whiteskunk, who replied:

"It's a human right to have good quality water, to have the earth beneath your feet, that you're tied to, which is also tied to the identity of Indigenous people, which is also incorporated into language. All of that is tied into human rights. When you take away human rights, that is a clear, blatant action, which demonstrates genocide."

Since the arrival of the first European settlers, Indigenous people have been confronted by forces determined to take away our land, and in turn destroy our culture. Yet we have survived and so have our cultures. We are still here. But as predicted at that 1977 United Nations conference in Geneva, climate change now threatens our way of life once again. This time, it is a threat to all who live on this planet. There are many Native American organizations and individuals across the United States fighting for the environment. And as we see the world begin to wake up to the threats of climate change, it is critical that political leaders and environmental activists alike look to Indigenous people for solutions to some of the world's most pressing problems, and that they work in concert with Native Americans rather than against us, as the United States has historically done.

Lopez-Whiteskunk says Indigenous people have been on the land for thousands of years, well before colonization, and we know how to take care of it. And she believes that the answers to climate challenges are embedded in that deep well of Indigenous knowledge.

Another element in that deep well of Indigenous knowledge is music.

# CHAPTER 14
## INDIGENOUS MUSICIANS
## AND STORYTELLERS

Music has been an intrinsic part of our culture for thousands of years. The drum represents the heartbeat of Mother Earth, and music has always been a way for us to heal, pray, and tell stories. If you listen to the rhythm in much of traditional Indigenous music, you'll notice the drum hits on every beat. Today, this rhythm is known as the "four on the floor," a reference to the drum hitting on all four beats of a measure. This rhythm is the backbone of much of the American blues, and roots music as the world knows it today. In the early- to mid-twentieth centuries, many people solely credited African Americans as the creators of the blues, a musical genre that would soon evolve into rock 'n' roll and, ultimately, today's American pop music. But most traditional African music is polyrhythmic, meaning it has multiple rhythms happening at the same time. Because of this, musicologists and historians in recent years have re-examined the origins of many of the key figures in the origin of the blues. And while the contributions of African Americans to the genre is undoubtable, the story of blues and rock 'n' roll wouldn't be complete without Native American musicians.

Charley Patton was one of the critical figures in the history of blues. Patton was a mixed African American and Native American (Choctaw) musician who personally taught Howlin' Wolf (also mixed Choctaw and African American) and many other international sensations how to play music and had a direct artistic influence on all American popular music that followed him.

When music historians do a side-by-side comparison of Charley Patton's recordings and the traditional Native American songs of the region, there is a stunning similarity in everything from vocal tone to the unique Native American rhythm patterns he implemented in his music. This came from the traditional Native American songs he grew up with.

Many of the most famous rock musicians of the last hundred years have mixed African American and Native American ancestry because our people's struggles within American society are intertwined, so our bloodlines, music, and stories are also deeply intertwined. A great example of this is Jimi Hendrix, credited today as one of America's greatest musicians.

Many people in the general public did not recognize his Native American ancestry because he was also African American. But in fact, Jimi's grandmother grew up on the reservation and was a vaudeville performer. According to his family, her work as a performer and her Native American upbringing had a profound influence on Jimi throughout his life. When you acknowledge this you start to see Jimi's references to his Native American ancestry throughout his career. For example, when he performed at Woodstock, a music festival held in upstate New York in 1969, where he wore a Native American fringe shirt with beadwork. Many people thought this was just the era of the hippies and he was representing the counterculture, which had already been pulling many things from Native American culture. But what Jimi was doing was expressing his unique cultural upbringing and what he believed gave him strength as a musician. You can also hear it in many of his lyrics where he oftentimes made direct references to Native people. Jimi wasn't the only Native American musician who performed at Woodstock and had a profound influence on American popular music.

Robbie Robertson, the primary songwriter and lead guitarist for the legendary rock band, the Band, is Mohawk, the same tribe as this author's family and Cayuga. Robbie and the Band are credited with changing the direction of rock music toward a fusion of roots, country, and rock music, creating the genre of music that we know today as Americana. Robbie Robertson grew up in Toronto, Canada, and his mother was from the Six Nations reserve (Haudenosaunee), where he would spend time with family that was all musicians, and at a young age, he caught the music bug. As a teenager, after teaching himself guitar licks relentlessly, he hit the road with the touring band Ronnie Hawkins and the Hawks, where he played alongside longtime collaborator and musical mentor Levon Helm. Eventually, Robbie and Levon left the Hawks and crossed paths with Bob Dylan in a New York City recording studio. At the time, Bob Dylan happened to be looking for a band to tour with him as he made his infamous transition from the world of folk music into the electrified world of rock 'n' roll. Robbie and Levon ended up touring the world with Bob Dylan.

In the years that followed, Robbie and Levon formed the Band, signed a record deal, and set up recording in a house in Woodstock, New York; the house was known as "Big Pink" for its bright pink exterior. Bob lived close by and often came over for songwriting and recording sessions. The rest, as they say, is history. Robbie is a monumental Native American figure who shaped the direction of rock music. But there was another Native musician who came before him who Robbie said was one of his greatest influences, and is considered one of the greatest influences on most modern rock guitarists today. This musician was Shawnee rockabilly legend, Link Wray.

Link Wray grew up in rural North Carolina and recalls as a child hiding underneath his bed as the Ku Klux Klan came to his family's property, targeting local Native American and Black families. Link Wray's mother was a Shawnee preacher who would travel to poor white, Native American, and Black communities, singing gospel songs with her kids, encouraging people to keep their heads held high in the face of rampant oppression and violence. Link Wray began to channel much of the pain and anger he experienced growing up into his music, and in 1958 released "Rumble," a song with no lyrical content but one of the most powerful guitar riffs anyone had ever heard. The song quickly became the only piece of purely instrumental music in history to be banned from US airwaves for fear of inciting youth violence. Today, "Rumble" is cited as the turning point in the evolution of modern rock guitar. Famous rock musicians such as Slash of Guns N' Roses, Iggy Pop, the MC5, the Black Keys, Taj Mahal, and Robbie Robertson all credit "Rumble" as one of their greatest influences. Link Wray's profound impact on the style, storytelling, and approach to rock 'n' roll guitar as we know it today is undeniable and solidifies in history the Native American influence on modern American popular music.

While we acknowledge the impact these rock stars have had, it is important to never forget the prolific contributions to the world of music that Indigenous women have also had. A major figure in the world of jazz in the 1930s was Mildred Bailey, who grew up on the Coeur d'Alene Reservation in Idaho. Mildred was one of the first women to have her own radio show. Her unique vocal style is cited by jazz legend Tony Bennett as being his single greatest influence. The glides and almost angelic high notes she was able to hit completely changed the direction of jazz singing. When music historians do a side-by-side analysis of Mildred's recordings and recordings of the traditional Native American songs of the region she grew up in, the similarity is mesmerizing. Once again, a Native American musician pulled influences from their upbringing and single-handedly changed music as we know it today. Not all Native American musicians made an impact by shaping the tone and style of the music itself, but they made profound social contributions that ignited a generation.

There is no greater example of this than Buffy Sainte-Marie, a Cree folk singer from Canada adopted into another Native family (her adoptive mother was of Mi'kmaq descent) and raised in Massachusetts. Buffy had a difficult childhood, suffering abuse from her older nonbiological brother, and talks about how creativity was a way for her to create a beautiful world of magic, wonder, and possibility as a small child; a place she could be completely enveloped in her imagination. In the Greenwich Village folk scene in New York City in the 1960s, when the world got wind of Buffy's music, people could not get enough. She became famous for her odd guitar tunings and beautifully vibrant song structures, but her career didn't stop there. She wrote the groundbreaking antiwar anthem of the time, "Universal Soldier," which addressed the brutality of the Vietnam war.

Buffy also publicly talked about the modern condition of Native Americans in a way that no popular musician of that era had done. And then, all of a sudden, her career seemingly came to an abrupt halt. It was only years later in interviews that she revealed that government programs issued by President Richard Nixon sent directives to radio stations across North America, secretly ordering the blacklisting of Buffy's music, effectively stopping her career dead in its tracks.

The struggle and oppression that popular Native American musicians had to endure is recognized now, and fits in with the widespread discrimination Native people have experienced in almost every facet of American life. Native musicians like Buffy, Robbie Robertson, Link Wray, and Jimi kicked down doors for all future Indigenous musicians and storytellers. Their struggle secured us a seat at the table.

We have always sung our song, and that can never be

taken away from us. Our story is unique and the places where we pull influences from are unique only onto themselves. They can criminalize our music, they can blacklist our artists, but the influence of Native Americans on popular music and other forms of media is undeniable—and we are only getting started.

The future is Indigenous. And it begins here with you.

# EPILOGUE
## A CLOSING NOTE FROM THE AUTHOR

In 2014, when I was in music school in Minneapolis–St. Paul, the newly elected mayor had run on a promise to change Columbus Day to Indigenous Peoples' Day. And as I sat in the Minneapolis American Indian Center, I witnessed a politician who had finally honored their promises to Indigenous people. The rush of emotions was a mixture of happiness and pride. It felt like I was witnessing something healing and changing in my community. I carry that memory with me everywhere I go. This would become the major turning point in my life that pushed me deeper into grassroots activism.